Read What These Christian Leaders Are Saying About Joe McGee

"I thought I had a lot to say in a short period of time until I met Joe McGee. Joe can pack more into one sermon or one book than anyone I have ever met. His insights into biblical parenting are unique and will open up scriptural secrets and common sense applications which will powerfully change your family. Don't miss the message of this book."

Reverend Bob Yandian
Grace Fellowship, Tulsa, Oklahoma

"No matter where you are in your parenting walk, this book will encourage and motivate you with practical, relevant and biblical keys that will bring parenting with purpose."

Eastman Curtis
Eastman Curtis Ministries

"What a rich source of godly counsel! Full of life, exuberant and filled with the Word of God, Joe McGee has become well known and highly esteemed by educators throughout the Christian school community.

"From elementary age kids to high school teenagers and their parents, Joe has the ability to communicate to all levels. His humor and zeal packs a powerful "Holy Spirit" filled punch. Joe is anointed with a message to encourage Christian parents who are raising kids in this postmodern age. He has a gift of giving insight into biblical principles, leaving no doubt that God's Word is applicable for Christian parenting today.

"I am very thankful that I can say that Joe, his wife Denise and their six children are the 'living testimony' of his message."

Dr. David B. Hand, Director
Oral Roberts University Educational Fellowship
International Christian Accrediting Association

"Joe McGee delivers some of the most entertaining, yet practical and insightful teaching on the family available today. Your family will never be the same after reading this book!"

Pastor David M. Blunt
Church on the Rock, St. Peters, Missouri

God Knows How To Raise Your Kids...
Even If You Don't

by

Joe McGee

Harrison House
Tulsa, Oklahoma

God Knows How To Raise Your Kids...
Even If You Don't!
ISBN 1-57794-032-6
Copyright © 1998 by Joe McGee
P. O. Box 691498
Tulsa, Oklahoma 74169-1498

Published by Harrison House, Inc.
P. O. Box 35035
Tulsa, Oklahoma 74153

Dedication

To Denise, the wife of my youth and my lifetime partner of twenty-five years, who loves me and inspires me to be a better father. I love you, honey.

And to Sarah, Jessica, Corrie, Tessa, Lauren and John — the six arrows God has placed in my quiver — who are specifically gifted as my personal instructors in parenthood.

Contents

Foreword

Dear Parents,

Here it is! Joe McGee has written a book to help you raise good Christian kids. And he's qualified! He's not only a gifted teacher and public speaker, he's a great dad. He and his family are part of our church and he has lived the things he shares in *God Knows How To Raise Your Kids... Even If You Don't!*

If you are really serious about raising your children to become disciples of Jesus Christ, you'll enjoy these teachings. Joe shoots straight from the hip and tells it like it is, but his message is soaked with compassion. You will gain new confidence in your role as a parent and find courage to steer your kids in the right direction – even when they offer resistance.

Your children are worth the time and the effort it takes to train them right. You won't have another chance, so let Joe McGee help you get it right. He knows what he's talking about.

Pastor Willie George
Church on the Move, Tulsa, Oklahoma

Introduction

When I was preparing to teach my very first class on biblical parenting, which I had entitled *The Origin of Children, or Where Do Babies Come From?*, I was using as a key text Psalm 127, verse 3, which says children are a reward from the Lord.

I thought to myself, *That has to be a mistake in translation. Everyone knows children cost parents not just time but money.* According to the *World Almanac*, the cost of raising a child is over ten thousand dollars per year. I thought, *Father, You've rewarded me enough! Why don't You reward someone else for a while?*

But then, as I was going through the book of Proverbs, I saw time and time again that children do bring rewards, and they are a reward. The thing is, the Bible has two distinct and different rewards for having children. One reward is positive, while the other is negative. One list of Scriptures tells how children bring happiness, joy and honor; another list tells how they bring sorrow, grief and shame. I thought, *Father, I have to find out how to get on that first list.*

I have realized over the years that producing the positive list of rewards involves more of what I do as a parent than what I try to get my kids to do. And since I myself am not a perfect parent, that really bothers me.

When I had just finished speaking to some sixteen hundred teenagers at a university, a group of young people came up to the stage and said, "Mr. McGee, we wish our dad was like you." That made me feel pretty good about myself; then I saw my oldest two daughters respond to that statement by rolling their eyes back in their heads and giggling.

I am not now, nor have I ever been, a perfect parent. But that's okay since perfection is not a prerequisite for having children. I am neither a famous child psychologist nor a behavioral expert.

So what were my reasons for writing this book?

First, because the Lord laid it on my heart long ago to do so; and second, because so many parents and pastors have asked me to do it. As I have conducted *Biblical Parenting 101* seminars across the country, I have frequently been asked, "Would you please put this information in a book?"

I can remember how the most valuable help and encouragement I received as a parent came during those early parenting classes that I taught in my local church, where I sat and visited with friends who also had children. I always left encouraged that I was not alone with wanting to train up my children different from the world. I was excited about what I was doing right and was determined to change what I was doing wrong.

As a parent of six, I desire that every parent come to know the truth from God's Word regarding the training up of their children. I also desire to put hope back in their lives. In this book I will be offering suggestions about parenting based on my own experiences as parent, school administrator and children's pastor.

How I have chosen to deal with my own situations as a parent may seem new to some. My experiences are offered to you, not as a means of bringing condemnation over any mistakes of your past, but for conviction that better ways of parenting be recognized and implemented. Each of us should be able to learn new parenting skills without being condemned over our past. We will then grow as a result.

It is the devil's job to be the accuser of the brethren. (Rev. 12:10.) As a parent, I know he tries to make me feel guilty for things I have done and haven't done, for things I have said and haven't said. That covers just about everything.

God's Word says that as believers we are the righteousness of God in Christ Jesus. (2 Cor. 5:21.) According to the book of Proverbs, the righteous may fall seven times a day. This Scripture says:

Proverbs 24:16 — **For a just man falleth seven times, and riseth up again....**

So what must the righteous do when they fall, when they make mistakes, when they miss it or when they just plainly commit a sin? They must get back up again! We should be known as the "getting-up people."

The world should be able to look at us, the righteous, and see the hope that is in us. But not because we are perfect; we aren't. They can see us going through the same tests and trials that they face. For some reason though, it seems we always come out smelling like a rose. We are like a cat that gets thrown in the air: it always lands on its feet. The world sees us like that and wonders why. We must give them the answer: His name is Jesus!

It's the wicked man, the Bible says, who falls down, refuses to get up and just wants to lie there. (Ps. 36:12.) Feeling sorry for himself and for his situation, the wicked man wants pity. But God is not moved out of pity. He cries when we cry, but He is moved only by faith. Faith comes from hearing the Word of God. (Rom. 10:17.)

Every subject in this book on parenting will be based on God's Word. I will be sharing some humorous stories from my experiences as well as practical ideas. What you read, you will be able to begin to use for yourself.

This won't change your family in twenty-four hours or in twenty-four days. I can't even promise it will change in twenty-four months. But it can turn the tide and put things back on the right path.

There is a standard we are to follow; it's called the Word of God. There are principles in God's Word that work, and we will be using them. As we delve into the subject of parenting, we will be covering a ton of Scripture, but it will be a practical study.

I call the subject, *Biblical Parenting 101*. There is no university you can attend where you will receive an education on biblical parenting. So consider yourself a new student who has just joined our class. I say to you, "Welcome to the class. Now let's begin."

1

Biblical Parenting

For many years parents have tried to raise their children based on what they saw others doing and what they learned by reading articles from magazines like *Reader's Digest* or *Good Housekeeping* or *Woman's Day*. They had a measure of success to some degree, but the answers that bring long-term solutions are found only in the Bible. These answers are there for those who will seek them out.

Many years ago when working in church as a children's minister, I discovered that, for some reason, parents considered the answer for their children to be church alone. They thought if they could just get their children to church, then somehow their kids would turn into spiritual giants. So every Sunday morning those children were sent off to church after having consumed and experienced God knows what throughout the previous week.

When I began my life as a parent, the only thing I knew about parenting was to tell children what not to do. As I had always heard it said, "You just can't tell children what not to do fast enough."

But I thought there just had to be more to parenting than saying no all the time. That's no fun; children don't like it, and neither do parents. Moms and dads can get hoarse from yelling at their kids so much, with their veins standing out and their blood pressure blowing up.

There just had to be a better way. I thought, *I refuse to live the way we've been living. We have to find a change somehow.*

"Teach Us About Parenting"

I remember one day talking with my pastor and saying: "Pastor, we have to find somebody to teach us young pups how to parent. With two toddlers right now, I don't know whether we're coming or going, and I don't see things getting any better in the future."

"That's a good idea, Joe. Then you need to find somebody, I guess."

"Well, I'll start looking," I said.

I spent the next three months hunting for someone there at our church who would be willing to teach a class on parenting. But no one would do it. The answer was always the same: "Why, I can't teach a class on parenting; I'm too busy working on my own children. Ask me again in ten years; maybe by then I'll know something."

Then I started looking for somebody with white hair. I thought anybody who had white hair was bound to have learned the ropes on parenting (assuming, of course, that person was not just prematurely gray!).

When I asked one lady about teaching the class, she looked at me and said, "Son, my baby is forty-five years old and I'm still working on him! I don't know anything about parenting."

At the end of those three months, I could see it was a fruitless endeavor, so I went back to the pastor and said, "Pastor, this is a hopeless situation. It's obvious that nobody feels qualified. We know now why we're in trouble."

Then he said, "Joe, that means you're just going to have to do it yourself."

"Well, I don't feel qualified either," I said, "but we'll give it a go."

So I sat down with my wife, Denise, and we talked about things we wanted to know as parents. We took out a pencil and a piece of paper and wrote down a list of forty-eight subjects for us to contemplate as topics in a class.

The first subject I wanted us to consider was the question, Where do babies come from? (And that was, in fact, the topic of our first class.) Other subjects about kids that we listed for possible discussion were thumbsucking, bedwetting, making good grades in school, lying, sex, dating, getting along with friends and the biblical discipline of children.

Class Begins

When we held this class for the first time, seventeen people showed up. We met at our church every Sunday for an hour before the evening service started. I would teach for about fifteen minutes; then we would talk with one another about that subject.

There were three tools I used in dealing with every subject: a Bible, a concordance and a book about that subject, which we would buy at a Christian bookstore. In preparing for the class, I wrote down every Scripture I could find.

Encouraging parents to use pencil and paper to take notes during the class, we began to build. We would briefly share at the beginning of class what the world was saying and doing about our subject, based on information we gathered from newspapers, books, magazines and the media. Then we would find out what God had to say in His Word, as well as share information from good Christian books on the subject. What God had to say was usually the opposite of everything we had ever heard or read from the world's point of view.

Our turnout for the class varied depending on which subject we were discussing. When we had classes on how parents were to teach their children about sex, I would have to bring in extra chairs. When I taught a class on child abuse, hardly anyone showed up. Other subjects covered were how to teach children about handling money and about picking their friends.

Called Into Full-Time Ministry

Together, Denise and I have spent the last twelve years teaching on the biblical principles of parenting.

About once a month somebody would call and say, "I know someone who goes to your church and I've heard about your teaching. Would you come over to our church and teach us on parenting?"

So we began traveling around to other churches. Then God separated us out full time.

I had been working as crusade coordinator for Willie George Ministries in Tulsa, Oklahoma. We had known Pastor Willie for several years and had taught at his children's workers camps and conferences.

Both he and my former pastor, Bob Yandian, at Grace Fellowship in Tulsa had chided me, saying, "If you don't steward this thing you are doing on parenting, God is going to take it away from you and give it to someone else."

Now, as the parent of six children, I have always been a homebody. When I am at home, I like to shut the gate and go into the house. I am not multi-social. So I was concerned, wondering, *How could I travel around the country teaching other parents about parenting if I am never able to spend time at home with my own family?*

Being troubled about it, I talked with my pastor, saying, "Pastor Willie, to do this, I'll have to always be leaving home. I don't like that."

"You just obey God, and He will take care of the rest," he said. Then he added, "But I don't think you'll have to be gone more than four or five times out of the month."

And that's exactly what has happened.

To be honest with you, I am home much more now than I ever was before. When I served as school administrator, it seemed I was never at home. I worked in the same building where my children attended classes, but I never saw them. So now I am able to see my children much more than before. They travel with me some of the time, and the older ones work part-time at our office.

Family Background

Let me give you a little information about our background. My wife, Denise, and I were childhood sweethearts. I never dated or kissed any other girl. It may seem like a strange situation, but that's just how it was. When you have found something good, there is no need to shop around. So we got married.

Both of our parents came from big families. There were twelve brothers and sisters in my father's family and five in my mother's, twelve in my father-in-law's family and six in my mother-in-law's. So when they got married, they had had enough of big families, of sharing everything from biscuits to pillows to clothes. My parents decided they only wanted one boy and one girl — and that's what they had, my sister and me. Denise's dad and mom had two boys and a girl.

But Denise and I grew up going to those large family reunions, and we both liked that. When we got married, we wanted a big family; in fact, we wanted five children. We decided to wait five years before beginning our family, and we did.

We asked God for five children, but since the Bible says in Ephesians 3:20 that God does above and beyond all we could ask or think, we got six! We ended up with five daughters and a son. Our last child was the boy.

Every Child Is Different

It's amazing how different children can be. About the time I thought I had learned how to raise our firstborn, she grew into another stage. It seems I could never quite catch her. Then our second child came along, another girl. By then I thought I had learned all about being a parent, but our second daughter was nothing like our first.

As a father when I am disciplining, I can give one of those ugly-face kind of looks. You know, something that looks like Attila the Hun raised from the dead. When I look at my firstborn in that way, she will respond immediately. But when I try using that same look on my secondborn, it sometimes seems to come back to me good measure, pressed down, shaken together and running over. Dealing with her requires a different approach.

That's true with every child. Each one is a little different.

Dwelling Together in Unity!

Now take six children and two adults, each having their own unique set of gifts and personalities; put them all under one roof and have them dwell together in unity. That is the miracle we call our family.

It takes work, and lots of it. Knowing that the devil's main tactic is to divide and conquer, we keep a constant vigil to make sure we don't let him in.

A classic example of how quickly things can suddenly get out of hand is the simple task of getting everyone ready to go to church.

It usually starts when I go to shave in the morning only to find my can of shaving cream empty because my toddlers used its entire contents the night before to take a bubble bath. After retrieving a new can from the pantry, I finally lather up. Then I take my razor and, with one quick swipe down my face, nick myself in ten different places. The reason: a dull razor! All six women in our house had used my razor the night before to shave their legs.

After having stopped the bleeding, I reach for my favorite toothbrush only to find that it has been knocked from its holder and is laying on the floor behind the toilet.

About this time, I learn that we have a typical Sunday morning math problem: too many women and not enough pantyhose! That requires a stop on the way to church at the convenience store to pay twice the price for another pair of hose. As the father of five daughters, I believe it is better to buy pantyhose by the pound than by the pair.

When we get everyone out of the house and into the Suburban, we suddenly remember that our vehicle was totally trashed during Saturday's all-day excursion to ball games, birthday parties, the grocery store, Wal-Mart and a trip to the vet.

By the time we finally make it to church, we need to sing praises to God.

But in those rare and precious moments when things are quiet and settled, we admit that we wouldn't trade this life for anything else in the world.

Practical Parenting

We will be dealing with many practical things in this study of biblical parenting. But you need to realize that there is no such thing as "seven methods" or "four ways" or "three types" of parenting.

Basically, there are two areas you need to deal with in parenting:

1. Attitude

2. Relationship

You have to get your attitudes and your relationships down pat. The rest is not that big of a deal. But you can only attain these attitudes and relationships by being a doer of the Word of God. (James 1:22.)

There is a key Scripture, found in the book of Luke, on which we will base this entire study. In describing the boy Jesus, this Scripture says:

Luke 2:52 — And Jesus increased in *wisdom* and *stature*, and in *favour with God and man*.

This verse could be said another way: that Jesus increased mentally, physically, spiritually and socially.

When any of these four areas are out of line in our lives, we will be faced with some challenges.

I don't think God left us down here on earth just to hang on. But having talked with so many parents across the country, I have heard them say, "We're just waiting for our children to turn eighteen and move out of the house."

If that's how we think, we need to realize that things will not automatically get better when our kids turn eighteen. We won't retire from parenting when that occurs; we will still be their parent when they get to be fifty-eight. If things aren't going well now and they won't automatically get better in the future, we need an attitude change.

Let's look again at Luke 2:52:

And Jesus increased in wisdom and stature, and in favour with God and man.

I believe God is very specific and detailed in His instructions to us. This Scripture gives four areas in which Jesus grew and developed in His life here on earth: in wisdom, in stature, in favor with God and in favor with man.

Let me give you four modern words to use for these four areas:

1. Wisdom = *Vision*

2. Stature = *Discipline*

3. Favor With God = *Stewardship*

4. Favor With Man = *Friendship*

In the following chapters we will examine each of these subjects in relationship to our children, describing ways in which they can grow and develop as Jesus did.

Wisdom = Vision

Luke 2:52 — **And Jesus increased in wisdom and stature, and in favour with God and man.**

The first subject in this verse of Scripture is *wisdom*. It says:

And Jesus increased in *wisdom*....

The word I will use for *wisdom* is *vision*. Jesus had a vision for His life.

The Bible says that Jesus only did what He saw the Father do and He only said what He heard the Father say. (John 5:19; 14:10.) Jesus knew where He came from, He knew why He was here and He knew where He was going. As He told His parents in Luke 2:49, "Don't you know I need to be about My Father's business?" He laid down His glory in heaven and took on the form of a servant. (Phil. 2:7.) As Hebrews 12:2 says, He endured the Cross for the joy that was set before Him. Jesus had a purpose for coming to this earth.

Children Frustrated With Life

Over the years, most of the family counseling problems I have dealt with involved the kids. These days so many children have no idea why they are here or where they are going, and they seem bored and frustrated with life.

These children are a classic example of the life described in Psalm 1, verse 1. This Scripture says:

Blessed is the man that walketh not in the counsel of the ungodly, nor standeth in the way of sinners, nor sitteth in the seat of the scornful.

Not only are today's children not walking with God, but they are walking in the counsel of the ungodly; in other words, following the advice and plans of the ungodly. After a while, they will begin standing in the way of sinners, meaning they will be hanging around sinners and submitting to their lead. Then after that, they will sit down in the seat of the scornful, resting and relaxing in a life of sin, complaining about everything and everybody.

As Jesus said, **Out of the abundance of the heart the mouth speaketh** (Matt. 12:34). After listening to a person for only five minutes, I will feel that I know him, because that which is in his heart will come out his mouth.

Most children are just frustrated with life. They say, "Life's a bum deal, and I've been dealt a bum hand." But that's a lie of the devil. The world is always trying to paint that idea into our children's minds. To them the grass is always greener on the other side of the fence.

Walking in Wisdom

Wisdom has several attributes, but let me just hit the high points for you. Let's look first in Proverbs 3:

Proverbs 3:13-15 — **Happy is the man that findeth wisdom, and the man that getteth understanding.**

For the merchandise of it is better than the merchandise of silver, and the gain thereof than fine gold.

She is more precious than rubies: and all the things thou canst desire are not to be compared unto her.

Then according to verse 16, if we are walking in wisdom, the benefits are excellent. It says:

Length of days is in her right hand; and in her left hand riches and honour.

With wisdom, three benefits will come to us while we are here on this earth:

1. We will live a long life.

2. We will have honor.

3. We will have wealth and riches.

Without wisdom, we will never have these three.

According to Proverbs 9:10, we can't have wisdom unless we have the fear of God. This verse says, **The fear of the Lord is the beginning of wisdom....**

If our children have no fear of God, they will have no wisdom, and they need wisdom to experience long life or honor or wealth and riches; and they will be struggling throughout this life.

We can do lots of good things for our children: We can send them to the best school, buy them the most expensive tennis shoes and sign them up to play on the best Little League baseball team. But their lives will still be miserable if they have no wisdom.

Every person is born with certain gifts and talents, which are given out at the moment of conception. As Scripture says, **the gifts and calling of God are without repentance** (Rom. 11:29). Your gift will make room for you; it can even make money for you. But if you have no wisdom, your life will be miserable; and true wisdom comes from the Word of God.

So, Jesus increased in wisdom; in other words, He had vision. This modern word, *vision*, is a good one. As Scripture says:

Proverbs 29:18 — **Where there is no vision, the people perish....**

Place God's Vision in Your Child's Heart

I want to paint a broad picture of vision in your mind.

As a parent (whether single or married; it makes no difference) our number-one job is to place God's vision in our child's heart. The world won't do it. Grandma won't do it. Our neighbors won't do it. The school system won't do it. We, the parents, have to plant that vision within our child. We have to paint a picture in his heart of how God sees him. Scripture says, "As a man thinks in his heart, so is he." (Prov. 23:7.)

In other translations Proverbs 29:18 reads like this:

"Where there is no vision, the people dwell aimlessly."

"Where there is no vision, the people dwell carelessly."

"Where there is no vision, the people dwell in violence."

In other words, people who have no vision can get bent out of shape about life. They could beat up anyone who stands in their way: their husband or wife, their children, their relatives, their neighbors. These people want to fight against anything that moves; they are just mad about life!

The classic saying is, "I didn't ask to be born." Maybe even you have said it.

No one has ever asked to be born. But life is like riding on a roller coaster. You had better pull back the bar in your seat and hang on, because you are going on a ride through life that's filled with ups and downs.

Jesus had vision. He knew why He came and where He was going. Most children these days don't have any idea as to their future. It's up to us as parents to plant a picture about God in our child's heart. But how are we to do that?

Suppose every morning the world came to your house, knocked on your door and said: "We represent your state and your county. We're here just to let you know we want to be a blessing to your children. We plan to speak good words to them and bring good things into their lives for the rest of their days." That would be wonderful!

But it will never happen in this world! The devil is at work in the world, trying to take complete control over our children.

A Parent's Responsibilities

According to Romans 13:1-8, every person in a position of authority — and that includes a parent — has two responsibilities: to confront and punish that which is evil, and to praise that which is good.

This means as parents we are to confront that which is wrong in our children and teach them to repent. Then we are to praise that which is good in them.

It's our responsibility as moms and dads to be the number-one cheerleaders in our families. Nobody else will cheer our children the way we can.

I have to admit, praise doesn't come natural to me, so I have to work at it; whereas criticism comes easy. I could get up every morning and see plenty of things to get bent out of shape about. I don't have to look hard; those things are usually staring me in the face. Sometimes I have to work at finding things in my kids to praise.

God Designed Praise

God is the One Who created praise. According to Scripture, there are some strange creatures hanging around His throne in heaven just to praise Him. In the book of Revelation, it says these creatures have one job day and night. They cry out, **Holy, holy, holy, Lord God Almighty, which was, and is, and is to come** (Rev. 4:8).

Suppose someone walked up to God's throne and said to Him, "Say, Father, what's with all these strange creatures around here?"

"I made them to praise Me."

"Is that all they do?"

"Yes."

"Don't they ever take a break?"

"No."

"Are You going to let them stop after a few thousand years?"

"No, they will be praising Me forever."

"Don't they ever get tired?"

"No, they just keep praising Me."

It sounds good, doesn't it?

Well, as Scripture tells us, we are made in God's image. (Gen. 1:27.) That means if God needs praise, we need it, too.

Our Children Need Our Praise

Children are definitely seeking praise. They need to receive praise from their own parents. Without it, they will seek after praise from their peers for all the wrong things they do, like talking trash, vandalism or other types of rebellion. They will find praise somehow and somewhere. If righteous praise doesn't come from their parents, they will get unrighteous praise from some other source.

When we are doing our job as parents, our children are not nearly as likely to be swayed by peer pressure. But we have to work at it. I have to purpose in my heart that I am going to do right-eously by affirming my children with the Word of God.

We must constantly reaffirm within our children the vision God has of them. Like Abraham did, we are to call those things that be not as though they were. (Rom. 4:17.) If our kids are weak, we must say they are strong. We have to say what God says in His Word.

Training Is Vital to Success in Life

Proverbs 22:6 — **Train up a child in the way he should go: and when he is old, he will not depart from it.**

We will be looking into this Scripture in greater detail, but first let me point out one important fact.

As this verse says, we are to *train up our children;* but, instead of training them, we simply raise them. We feed them and clothe them. We give them their own room, their own car and boom box, and leave them to plan their own life. Then we wonder why they don't turn out any better. Training involves having in mind a specific end result. It is showing our children what to do and then seeing to it that they do it.

Training is vital to success in life. Let me give a couple of examples.

When I went away to Army basic training, I was placed under the authority of a drill sergeant. I was taken away from my mother, my girlfriend, my chocolate donuts and my TV. All the hair was removed from my head, my civilian clothes were taken away and I was dressed in a green uniform. Then I was put in a room with 120 other guys. I had to get up at crazy hours and couldn't go to bed when I wanted to. I was in training. But the more training I received and the quicker I was able to perform, the sooner I began to enjoy some freedoms.

I remember an experience my dad had trying to raise tomato plants. He raised some of the most delicious and beautiful tomatoes in the Tennessee Valley. But that wasn't always so. In the beginning he wasn't very good at it.

A little bud would come up on the vine, and a nice tomato would be ripening. But when Dad went out to pick it, the vine would be laying over on the ground under the weight of the tomato — and the worms had beaten him to it!

Then one day an elderly neighbor came by and said, "Mr. McGee, you need to train those plants. We'll get some wire mesh and put some around it." So he came back later, pulled up the old plants and put up the wire mesh. Then Dad started all over again with some new plants.

When the plant began to bud and little tomatoes came out, the pressure of the new green tomatoes began to pull the plant over to one side. So Dad took some twine, tied it around the stem and gently pulled it back in line. When pressure drew it the other way, he pulled it back in the opposite direction. He kept straightening the neck of that little stem until he could grow tomato plants four feet tall and was producing fruitful crops. Those tomatoes could be eaten because the plants had been trained to grow and produce.

During the time of training, parents can get an idea of where the end is. But they have a problem: they don't look at the end; they are always looking at "right now," saying, "Things aren't good now and I'm mad." They need to be looking at the end result. Remember, God calls those things that be not as though they were. (Rom. 4:17.)

Most drivers' training manuals will tell you that the best way to stay straight while driving on the highway is not to look directly across the front hood of your car but to look at a fixed point down the road. Keep your eyes looking ahead, where you want to go, not just where you currently are.

God Sees the End Result

When the Angel of the Lord came down from heaven seeking Gideon, He said to Gideon, **The Lord is with thee, thou mighty man of valour** (Judg. 6:12).

Gideon's response shows us that he didn't see himself that way. Gideon was a man without a vision; he saw himself as weak, poor and unable to do anything about his situation. He looked up as if to say: "Angel, you must have made a wrong turn in heaven. My name is Gideon. I'm the youngest member of my family, and we're the poorest of our tribe. The Lord has left us and we've been taken captive. Things are hopeless and the people here are starving to death." (Author's paraphrase; see vv. 13,15.)

But the Lord's response reveals how He saw Gideon by faith: **Surely I will be with thee, and thou shalt smite the Midianites as one man** (Judg. 6:16). God did not call Gideon what he was; for by Gideon's own admission, he was a wimp hiding in a hole. God called him what he was going to become.

God doesn't see what we are; He sees what we will become. That's how we, as parents, are to see our children. I don't look at my children for what they are. Right now they may be klutzy. I see them, not for what they are, but for what they will become.

The Bible talks in the gospel of Luke about how Jesus stayed up all night praying, talking to the Father. He was getting ready to select the twelve disciples He would name as apostles. (See Luke 6:12-16.)

As Jesus said, He only did what He heard the Father say, so I can imagine the conversation going something like this:

"Okay, Father, who are We going to pick as My disciples?"

"The first one will be James."

"Oh, that's good, Father. I like James. He's a good, solid businessman. Who's next?"

"I want You to pick Matthew."

Jesus thinks a minute, then says, "There are lots of Matthews. Which one do You mean?"

"You know the one."

"Oh, Father, You don't mean that tax collector, do You?"

"That's the one."

"But, Father, I can't have a tax collector following Me. I mean, things are bad enough with the ministry as it is. People like that are hated and spit upon."

"Take Matthew."

So Jesus says, "Not My will, but Thy will be done." After writing down the names of James and Matthew, He asks, "Who's next?"

"I want You to pick Peter."

Jesus thinks a minute, then says, "Peter? Father, there are several guys named Peter. Which one do You have in mind?"

"You know the one."

Jesus cringes for a moment, then says, "Father, You don't mean that big, loudmouthed fisherman, do You?"

"That's the one."

"But, Father, he has the trashiest mouth. He cusses and has a hot temper. I can't have him following Me around in the ministry."

"Pick Peter."

Again, Jesus says, "Not My will, but Thy will be done," and He adds Peter's name to the list.

The twelve apostles were some of the klutziest guys ever put together at one time.

Using New Testament street talk, Jesus had said to them: "How long do I have to put up with you guys? When are you going to get some faith? I can't hang around here forever; I have to go home! You need to get hold of this." (Author's paraphrase; Mark 9:19; 4:40.)

Then two of the disciples, James and John, who were called the **sons of thunder** (Mark 3:17), brought their mother to Him to get permission for them to sit on either side of Him in glory. They were concerned more about a title and position than about ministry. (See Matt. 20:20,21.)

But these twelve klutzy guys are the same ones God used in three and one-half years to turn the world upside down. They worked at evangelizing the whole known world.

So, as parents we must have patience with our sometimes klutzy kids. God looks at things differently from the way we do. Looking down through time, He sees the end result; He calls us, not what we are, but what we will become.

3

Painting the Vision

Let's consider the stories of Joseph and Daniel, two of my favorite Bible characters. Their parents had planted some truth inside them, and they had a vision of who they were and of what they were to do.

Both Joseph and Daniel ended up in a foreign country under the leadership of heathens. They were people of the wrong color from the wrong culture who spoke the wrong language and practiced the wrong religion. In these strange lands, they had no family, no friends, no finances. Yet both of them were given great authority over those heathens.

Do you know what was said about Daniel under King Darius? Scripture says, **...an excellent spirit was in him; and the king thought to set him over the whole realm** (Dan. 6:3). Now Darius, being a heathen, didn't know God and didn't care to know Him. But he saw something special in Daniel; he just didn't know what it was. Yes, there *was* "something special" about Daniel: it was the Spirit of Almighty God at work in his life!

There were three heathen kings who, one after the other, had run that country, and Daniel sat under their regimes. Each of those kings saw the good job Daniel could do, so he was put in a position of authority and kept in charge.

I want you to realize that there can be this kind of promotion in our children's lives too. With the Spirit of God inside them, they can walk out into the world and be blessed as they follow God's plan and purpose for their lives.

That's what I want for my children. I want them to achieve everything God has for them, whether living under my roof or going out into the world. Wherever they are, I want God to look at them and speak those beautiful words: "Well done, thou good and faithful servant." (See Matt. 25:20,21.)

A Godly Seed

In dealing with children, no two of them are the same. As stated in Psalm 127, verse 3, our children are a reward from God.

But, Mom and Dad, you will never hear from the world that children are a reward from God. Instead, you will read how they cost you so much money and take up so much of your time.

Through the book of Proverbs, there are two lists of rewards which having children will bring to us. One list is positive and one is negative. Our children can bring us blessing, honor, peace and prosperity; or they can bring grief, sorrow, shame and dishonor.

"Which reward am I going to get, God?"

"That is entirely dependent upon you, son."

According to the book of Malachi, God isn't looking just for a seed, but for **a *godly* seed** (Mal. 2:15).

Take my word for it: Having six kids doesn't make you holy. It could drive you insane or keep you broke if you don't know and do the Word of God.

If you read through the Bible, you will see that there were times when God specifically got involved in children being born; but it was rare. Some people never married; others were married but never had kids. Some got married and had only one child, while others had twelve or more.

Sometimes God was very detailed, telling certain people that they would have x-number of kids. But ninety-nine percent of the time, God was saying to His people: "When you sow human seed, you will reap human crop. You can have as many children as you want. There will be plenty of children and plenty to feed them, for I have never seen the righteous forsaken nor their seed begging bread." (See Deut. 28:11; Ps. 37:25.)

My Seed Shall Be Mighty

One of the required courses at our school, called "Biblical World View," involved the students selecting a single subject of their choosing, which could range anywhere from politics to sports.

Each class period, the students cut at least one article from the daily newspaper to be kept in a scrapbook. At the end of each nine weeks, they condensed those forty-five articles into a one-page summary report. At that time they were given one week, using their Bible, a concordance and a dictionary, to find a minimum of twenty-five Scriptures also about that subject, condensing them into a one-page summary report. They then had to give a five-minute oral report comparing the two summaries.

The purpose? To show that, regardless of what subject they picked, whatever the world had been saying about that subject for the last nine weeks, God had been saying almost the exact opposite for the last four thousand years.

One student had picked the subject of overpopulation and had cut out articles about how we were running out of food, water, oil and land, as well as how the ozone layer around the earth is being depleted. Yet in his research of the Scriptures, he discovered in Revelation 20:6 that there is to be at least a thousand-year reign of our Lord Jesus Christ on this *existing* planet — not on a new planet. That means, unless we have missed the Rapture of the church, when Jesus comes to take us to be with Him in heaven, there must be at least a thousand-year supply of food, water, gasoline and ozone on this planet.

Now it's a fact that humans are abusing this planet. That's what sin does: it abuses. But even with all the abuse that occurs, there are still plenty of supplies left.

Many times I have had people say to me, "But, Joe, aren't you concerned about your children growing up in today's world? Who will be out there for your children to marry? There aren't going to be any virgins left on this planet. Everybody will be dying of AIDS!"

"No, they won't," I say. "I have five daughters and a son, so there are five godly young men and a godly young woman somewhere out there who are still virgins and are being trained up for my children."

Then I quote God's Word to them. I say about my children what God's Word says in Psalm 112. (You have to choose what you are going to believe for yourself. Don't look to your neighbors or your friends; look to God's Word.)

Psalm 112:1,2 — **Blessed is the man that feareth the Lord, that delighteth greatly in his commandments.**

His seed shall be mighty upon earth: **the generation of the upright shall be blessed.**

"Big deal," they say. "Maybe each of your children will find a good godly spouse who is a virgin, but they'll have to work two or three jobs between them just to live. With so much inflation, a normal house will cost three hundred thousand dollars."

"I don't care if houses cost a million dollars," I say. "If I fear God and delight in His commandments, blessings will come to my children. As Psalm 112:3 says, they will have wealth and riches in their house."

"Okay, so what if your kids do get wealthy?" they say. "I have seen marriages fall apart."

"Yes, it can happen," I say. "But God is the great Redeemer and Restorer."

Psalm 112, verse 4, says, **Unto the upright there ariseth light in the darkness....** If we will just hang tough and stand on His Word, God promises to show up on our behalf.

Speaking a Vision

I remember how I had to hang tough after I was called into the ministry. The testimony I will share is a good example of how important it is for us to speak a vision into other people's lives, especially our children's.

I had been working in the wire manufacturing business for eight years when my wife and I decided to attend a Bible school in another state. So we had to pack all our belongings for a move to Oklahoma.

Just three days before we were scheduled to leave, I was offered a job transfer to West Virginia with a big raise. The promotion I had always wanted was dropped in my lap. That's how the devil will work, trying to sidetrack us. But we refused to be sidetracked from our destination, either spiritually or physically.

We packed up everything we owned, filled the back of a large U-Haul truck and headed for Broken Arrow, Oklahoma, a suburb of Tulsa.

When we got there, we checked into a motel. I just picked out Howard Johnson's as we were driving down the highway. Then I went to a real estate agency to see about a place to live.

When I walked in, I said to the real estate lady, "We're looking for a house to rent. We've been believing God for a three-bedroom with a garage and a fence around the backyard." (I was very specific with my description, because the more specific you are with God, the more specific He is with you.)

Our conversation lasted maybe thirty seconds. She said, "No, we don't have anything. With Bible school starting, the city is packed. You probably won't find anything."

And we didn't! There were no houses or apartments to rent, and there didn't appear to be any jobs available. We couldn't even find a place to store our furniture. I had just twenty-four hours to turn in the rental truck.

Back at the motel, my wife and I were sitting there in the room feeling as if we had really missed God. It was a hot summer day, and I was discouraged. I thought, *I have left behind my whole career — everything! I thought I was following God, and God isn't even here. What are we going to do now?*

Denise was looking at me, and I just sat there with tears in my eyes, wondering, *What have I led my family into?* I had been down on my face interceding until there were rug burns on my forehead!

Finally, I called back home to my pastor. In misery, I cried out: "Pastor, I missed God! I just don't know what's happening! God isn't here, and I don't know how I missed Him. I'm going to West Virginia to get my job back."

But my pastor said, "Now wait, Joe; you need to be quiet a minute."

Then his wife, Arnelle, got on the phone. She said: "Joe, I'll tell you what we're going to do: we're going to pray for the Lord to send the angels out and just get you a place right now, in Jesus' name."

When she said that, I thought to myself, *Gee, my pastor's wife is a real flake!*

Denise could hear my end of the conversation. I was saying, "Really? Really? Okay, Arnelle, angels are going to get me a house. Fine. Well, praise God."

Just as people do sometimes, I was agreeing with Arnelle as much as I could and sounding better to her than I really felt inside.

When I hung up the phone, I flipped my chair around, sat down and rested my feet on the side of the bed.

I saw that Denise was putting some things in her pocketbook, so I asked, "What are you doing?"

"Well, if the angels are going to get us a house, we have to put some feet to this faith. We have to go."

"I'm not going anywhere," I said. "Arnelle said the angels of God would have us a house in the next twenty minutes. If I'm going to work for God and follow Him, then He had better do something now, or I'm not going anywhere with Him."

I said it just like that. I noticed one of those battery-operated clocks hanging on the wall, so I sat there in that chair just watching the clock.

Denise must have thought, *My husband has gone crazy! I thought I had a man of God who was leading us someplace.*

Then she said, "Don't you think we ought to at least make some calls — or something?"

"I'm not calling anybody," I said. "If God is God, He needs to show up now. He said for us to test Him, so I'm testing Him. He said to prove Him, so I'm proving Him."[1] Then I said, "God, You had better do something right now."

As I sat there watching that clock, seventeen minutes went by. Then, all of a sudden, the phone rang.

I thought, *Who in the world knows I'm here at Howard Johnson's?*

When I answered, it was the real estate lady I had talked with when we first came to town. I don't even remember telling her we were staying at Howard Johnson's, but evidently I had.

She said, "Is this Mr. McGee who came into our real estate office day before yesterday?"

"Yes, it is. Who is this?"

---

[1] MALACHI 3:10 NAS, KJV.

After identifying herself, she said: "You're not going to believe this, but I just got a call. A house has opened up in Broken Arrow. I wondered if you were interested."

"What kind of house?" I asked.

"Well, it's a three-bedroom with a garage. It has a fence on three sides, but they're getting ready to put up a fence on the fourth side, and it's in the same block as the Bible school. Would you like to look at it?"

"Yes, I think we'll come over and take a look at it," I said.

I never laugh at anybody anymore when they start praying for me. I say, "Lord, I believe; just help my unbelief." (Mark 9:24.)

I have learned that sometimes it takes other people to speak a vision into our lives. So now I know the importance of speaking a vision into my children's lives.

I want to share two stories now, one telling about the bigness of God and another telling about the smallness of God.

How Big God Is

Sometimes we don't think God is big enough to do anything for us, so let me tell you how big God is.

My kids take part in the science fair at our school, which is an eventful time of the year. While they are working on their projects, our house gets turned into trash for about seven days, and it looks like a tornado has run through it. Their projects have included growing plants and creating funguses. It's a weird time of the year, but we survive it.

My older daughter was interested in astronomy, so during her project we were looking at the sun, the planets and their moons. I discovered just how amazing our universe is. It's a big place!

Through the use of the Hubble Space Telescope, we are able to see things we didn't even know existed. There are some 50 billion known galaxies out in space, and we live in one of them, the Milky Way, which is among the smallest of all those galaxies. If you go out at night, you can look up and see the Milky Way. The galaxies are hundreds of thousands of light years apart.

There are some 30 billion suns in our galaxy alone. The sun in our solar system is one of the smallest of those 30 billion, yet the earth is a million-and-a-half times smaller than our sun.

Now when I was growing up, I had a tough time trying to figure out what God looked like.

I remember asking my dad such questions as: "What does God look like? Does He have a long beard and white hair? What does He do all day long? Does He ever get bored?"

"No, son, God isn't bored; He's just there. Remember He told Moses, 'I AM THAT I AM.'"[2]

I heard Dad say that to me, but it didn't really register. So then I asked him, "Well, when was God born?"

"He wasn't born, son; He just is."

"But everybody has to be born, Dad. We have to start somewhere."

"No, son, God never started."

I once read an article about the space shuttle, which commented: "We are very pleased with the space shuttle program, except for one thing: We wish we could design it to achieve the speed of light. If it could achieve the speed of light, we could do some long-range space exploration."

Scientists discovered years ago that at the speed of light, or 186,000 miles per second, time would cease to exist in space. On a space mission traveling at that speed, an astronaut could take forty years going out and forty years coming back. When back on

---

[2] EXODUS 3:14.

the earth, he wouldn't have aged while the people here would be eighty years older.

Let me give you an idea of how fast that is. Let's say you point a .22 rifle into the air and pull the trigger. If that bullet traveled at the speed of light — 186,000 miles per second — it would have circled the earth seven times before you even took your finger off the trigger.

Now, lining this up with the Word of God, the Bible says that God is Light. (1 John 1:5.) That's why there is no time in heaven; everything just is.

My dad, who was a real character, always had to be on time. He was always looking at his watch, saying, "What's the schedule? What time is it? Where are we going?"

So after he went home to be with the Lord, the kids were saying: "Can you just imagine Grandpa getting up this morning in heaven? He doesn't have a watch, so that's driving him nuts. He must be rubbing his wrist raw, thinking, *What are we doing today?*"

Let's suppose there was a conversation between two people in heaven, going something like this:

"Well, how long have you been here?"

"Oh, about 1,400 years."

"Well, I've only been here 22 days. I'm just getting used to the place."

People in heaven are not aware of time. Heaven has no concept of time — no sun, no moon, no yesterday, no tomorrow. I would call heaven an "is" place.

Now let me tie all of this together. I want you to realize how big God is.

Let me tell you, in our own galaxy — the Milky Way, the smallest of all the 50 billion galaxies we know about — there are 100,000 light years from one side of it to the other.[3]

---

[3] *The ABC's of Nature* (Pleasantville, New York: Reader's Digest Assn., 1984), p. 11.

Let's say, for example, I could get into my pickup truck, leave this earth and cruise up into space. If I kicked it into high gear, traveling at 186,000 miles per second, it would still take me 100,000 years to go from one side of our galaxy to the other, and our galaxy is the smallest.

How big is it out in space? Our brain will never reach there, and we can't even think of it. It's big — even bigger than Texas! And it took no effort for God to create it; He is even bigger than that!

How Small God Is

Now let's consider the science of DNA. There has been much talk in recent years about the use of DNA in catching criminals. I will try to paint a picture of this.

At the moment of conception, when the sperm and egg come together, the first thing that's created is a fertilized egg cell in which is found a little twisted chain of molecules of DNA. It's like a little guy with a clipboard who writes down a description of all the cells in the body. It's called the body's blueprint. It would be his job to tell each of them what they are to do as they come into existence. He says to them: "I want you two trillion cells to line up over here. You four million, go over there. You twenty-two need to be over here, and you five should go over there."

Everything about our physical anatomy is planned out at the moment of conception. Our hair color, our eye color, our nose size, how knobby our knees are — all of it can be found in the DNA.

God, the Creator, went into that much detail in creating our physical body, going down to even the minutest of molecules as a basis to form the entire human being. God put us on this tiny planet engulfed in a universe so big that a computer would burn out trying to cover it all.

God Has Big Plans for His Kids

Did God, Who made us and placed us in a universe so large we cannot conceive of its limitless size and in a body which at its conception was blueprinted down to the smallest detail, leave us here in between to run around like a rat in a maze in this thing called life?

If that were true, He might have said, "Well, I got them started. Now I'll see how they make it. Oops! There they go bumping into something."

But God didn't leave us here on our own.

The Bible says the steps of a righteous man are ordered of the Lord. (Ps. 37:23.) Nobody else except you and me, as parents, are better qualified to plant inside our children the vision of how big God is and how small He can become to reach them right where they are.

Remember, God called to the apostle John on the isle of Patmos and said to him, **...Come up hither, and I will shew thee things which must be hereafter** (Rev. 4:1). Then John was taken up into heaven and shown things of the future.

If you can imagine, God is sitting at the center of existence where there is no time; and in our universe, time revolves around Him. Where we are, time is; where God is, there is no time.

God tells John to watch while events are taking place. As John is writing down all that he sees, he must be thinking, *Wow! That's really something!* The things he sees hadn't happened yet; he is seeing them as they are occurring.

Don't miss this point: All that John saw hadn't happened yet; he was watching as those events were taking place before him.

That's why Jesus, speaking of the Holy Spirit, said: **Howbeit when he, the Spirit of truth, is come...he will shew you things to come** (John 16:13). Why? Because He is God.

46

God knows what we are going to do two minutes from now, two days from now, two months from now, two years from now. God has good plans for His children.

When Israel was being taken captive in Babylon, God was saying to them: "Boys, I know it doesn't look good, but this wasn't My plan. The plans I have for you aren't meant to harm you but to prosper you. I have plans to give you a future and a hope." (Author's paraphrase; see Jer. 29:11-14.)

You need to realize that the world is lying when it says, "God did that to you!" God didn't do it; the devil did it, or the world's system did it, or maybe your own flesh did it.

When God called Jeremiah as His prophet, Jeremiah was half-scared. He was saying, "Lord, I don't know if I can do this." But God was saying: "Yes, you can, son. Stop your knees from knocking. Just be still and listen to Me. Before I ever made heaven and earth, I knew your name." (Author's paraphrase; see Jer. 1:4-8.)

Even if you don't know who your parents are, God knows your name and He has a plan for your life. You need to realize that nobody ever catches God off guard. He has a divine blueprint for your life. He says, "I know the plans I have for you. They are good plans to prosper you and to give you a future and a hope." Do you believe that?

Change Comes a Little at a Time

You have to plant a vision in your children: a true vision of what God thinks about them and what kind of future He has planned for them. You do it with words that come from the Scriptures, and they come a little at a time. As God's Word says in the book of Isaiah:

Isaiah 28:9,10 — **Whom shall he teach knowledge? and whom shall he make to understand doctrine? them that are weaned from the milk, and drawn from the breasts.**

For precept must be upon precept, precept upon precept; line upon line, line upon line; here a little, and there a little.

Listen to me, Mom and Dad: You do things a little at a time. I don't care what your family situation may be. It's a circumstance, and maybe even a bad one, but circumstances can change — no matter how hopeless they may look. I don't care if your children are adults, the situation can still change.

When Jesus was preaching all those great sermons at the age of thirty-three, there were probably some mamas sitting around, listening to Him and saying, "Where were You thirty years ago?"

I know; I have been in situations like that.

After hearing the truth preached, don't just say, "That's great! I wish I'd heard that a long time ago." Instead, say, "Thank God, I've heard the truth today! Now I know how to pray for my children."

When praying for your children, ask God to enlighten the eyes of their understanding. Pray that He send laborers across their path and loose the Spirit of God to bring conviction to their hearts. Boldly say, "I command that blindness be removed from my children's minds and eyes, in Jesus' name!"

You have to do righteously concerning your relationship with your children. Pray for the Lord to give you wisdom on how to handle them and talk with them. If you will do righteously toward them, God will honor it.

There is no situation that God can't turn around. Not one! If your family has split apart, He can bring all of you back together again. If you have a good family, He can make it a great family. Jesus came to redeem and to restore.

All that's needed is for you to come together in agreement with God. No person, no flesh and no demon in hell can stand against you!

Say What God Says

The world is always lying to you. You will hear how hopeless everything is. You will be told stories of how people who are just like you bit the dust and didn't get up. But don't feed on that!

Say what God's Word says: "A thousand may fall on one side of me and ten thousand on the other side, but it won't come near me! My home may look like it's falling in, but God's Word says no evil shall come nigh my dwelling." (Author's paraphrase; see Ps. 91:7,10.)

In Luke 6, Jesus told about two kinds of houses: those built on the rock and those built on the sand. (vv. 46-49.) My house is built on the rock of the Lord Jesus Christ. But does that make me immune from life and its circumstances? No! God is saying, "The storms of life will beat vehemently against your house, Joe McGee, but it won't fall."

The Williams' New Testament[4] says:

Luke 6:47,48 — Everyone who comes to me and continues to listen to my words and practices their teaching, I will show you whom he is like. He is like a man who was building a house, who dug deep, and laid its foundation upon the rock; and when a flood came, the torrent burst upon that house but it could not shake it, because it was well built.

God never said the storms wouldn't come. As He said through the prophet Isaiah:

Isaiah 43:2 — When thou passest through the waters, I will be with thee; and through the rivers, they shall not overflow thee: when thou walkest through the fire, thou shalt not be burned; neither shall the flame kindle upon thee.

---

[4] CHARLES B. WILLIAMS, THE NEW TESTAMENT: A PRIVATE TRANSLATION IN THE LANGUAGE OF THE PEOPLE (CHICAGO: MOODY PRESS, 1956).

We may have tough experiences throughout our lives, but we can walk in victory and keep coming out on the other side like someone who has been raised from the dead.

People will look at us and, with their jaws dropping open, they will say, "How did they turn that situation around?"

We can tell them the answer, saying: "His name is Jesus! He turned that situation around in my life."

You have to determine that you are going to say and do what the redeemed of the Lord says and does. If you are looking and feeling weak, you have to say to God: "I may look and feel like a dog that was run over and then backed over again, but I say I'm strong, Lord!"

God will respond, "That's all I want you to say, son. You do your part and I will do My part."

When the Israelites reached the Red Sea, Moses may have thought, *Oh, we're in trouble now!* But God said, "Hold up that stick, Moses, and I will part the water." (Author's paraphrase; see Ex. 14:16.)

When God's people came to the big walls of Jericho, God said to Joshua, "Have the men to walk around the city seven times, and I will knock it down." They did, and He did! (See Josh. 6.)

Take Authority Over Your Home

If you apply the Word of God to your life, God will perform His Word. (Isa. 55:11.) But you need to *do* it so that God can work on your behalf.

Now in the midst of your turmoil, He will cry with you, saying: "I know it's bad; I feel bad too. But if you will do something, if you will speak My Word and believe that I will bring it to pass, I will help you."

Our heavenly Father saw His Son Jesus being spat upon, beat to the point of being unrecognizable and nailed to a cross. But now Jesus sits at the right hand of the Father, interceding for your children and mine. (Rom. 8:34.) God loves our children more than we will ever be able to love them.

If you even whisper a prayer to God, He will knock down some fences and kick some demons from pillar to post! When you ask Him from your heart, He will move in your behalf.

There is just one important requirement for you to fulfill as a parent: You must be taking authority in your home. You didn't become a parent because you are the most qualified. You aren't head of your home because you have the highest intelligence or the most degrees. You are there by divine appointment. So you have to stand up and take your authority. Don't let the devil put you down.

You might ask, "How can I judge my child for doing something wrong when I do the same thing myself?" That's why Luke 6:40 in *The Amplified Bible* says that a pupil, when fully taught, will be just like his teacher. Our children do what we do, not just what we say. That means we have to be growing in the grace and knowledge of our Lord Jesus Christ, becoming more like Him every day.

That's our responsibility as a parent. We stand in that place of authority, not because we are sinless, but because God has put us there. That's why we have to be quick to repent whenever we do wrong.

When we know we have sinned, it takes only about five seconds to ask forgiveness and to be cleansed. As the Scripture says:

1 John 1:9 — **If we confess our sins, he [the Father] is faithful and just to forgive us our sins, and to cleanse us from all unrighteousness.**

As the head of my home, I stand washed and cleansed, not because I have lived a perfect life, but because I am forgiven through the blood of Jesus.

My kids know I am not perfect. I sometimes mess up on a consistent basis, but I have learned to repent in front of them. It's hard to do sometimes, but I say, "Hon, I'm sorry. That was a stupid thing I said and a dumb thing I did. Will you forgive me?" Then I have to ask God to forgive me. I'm going to keep growing in God's grace and knowledge.

There is strength in that, not because I have a perfect past, but because I have a perfect God. It's the grace of God being sufficient in me. His name is Jesus, and you can lean on Him, too.

My Prayer for You and Your Family

I want you to get a picture in your mind of all your loved ones — your spouse, your children, your grandchildren. While you are picturing them, I will tell you how Jesus prayed in John 17. He said: "Father, I pray not only for those who are alive today but for all those yet to be born." (Author's paraphrase; v. 20.)

Jesus prayed three things, and I want to pray them for your family right now:

Heavenly Father, I pray that Mom and Dad will be a tremendous influence over their family.

Number one, I pray what Jesus prayed: that You make them one together as members of the Body of Christ, just as You and Jesus are One. May there be unity in this home. May these parents and their children walk as close to You as did Your Son Jesus. If it were not possible, He would not have prayed it. So may they continue to grow in Your grace and in Your knowledge.

Number two, Father, let the joy of Jesus be manifested in their lives. Let these parents and their children be known as families of laughter and of joy.

Number three, Father, Jesus said the world would hate all believers because they are not of this world, and He prayed that they not be taken out of this world but be kept from the evil in it. So I pray now,

Father, that You keep this family from the evil that's in this world, in Jesus' name.

A Prayer You Should Pray for Your Children

There are three things you should pray for your children this year. They are:

1. *Father, I thank You for teaching my children to fear, or reverence, You.*

   As Psalm 34:11 says:

   Come, ye children, hearken unto me: I will teach you the fear of the Lord.

   If your children fear God, it's the beginning of wisdom. With wisdom, they will have long life, honor and riches.

2. *Father, surround my children with a shield of divine favor.*

   Psalm 5:12 says:

   For thou, Lord, wilt bless the righteous; with favour wilt thou compass him as with a shield.

   This is saying that the Lord will surround the righteous with a shield of divine favor wherever they go. It can cover their teachers, the neighborhood kids and their employer.

   As an employee, you can pray, "Father, I thank You that I have divine favor. I pray that the heathen will like me and not even know why." This is a promise from God.

3. *Father, I ask You to send good friends to my children — godly friends who will sharpen them like iron and cause them to be all You want them to be — and cut away any friends who would drag them down.*

   Proverbs 27:17 says, **Iron sharpeneth iron; so a man sharpeneth the countenance of his friend.**

You should say this in a prayer of thanksgiving every morning, saying, "Father, I thank You...."

When I get up in the morning, I pray: "Father, I thank You for my kids — Sarah, Jessica, Corrie, Tessa, Lauren and John. I believe You are teaching them to fear You. You are surrounding them with a shield of divine favor. You are giving them godly friendships that will sharpen them like iron, making them a mighty man or woman of God. I thank You for doing it in Jesus' name."

God wants to do that for our children. So make this your prayer confession for them, and then thank Him for it.

4

Stature = Discipline

Luke 2:52 — And Jesus increased in wisdom and stature, and in favour with God and man.

I want us to look now at the second part of this Scripture verse, which says:

And Jesus increased in...*stature*....

One commentary says, "Jesus matured physically and mentally."[1]

The word I want us to use for *stature* is *discipline*.

To grow in stature means Jesus had some discipline, or self-discipline, about Himself. As He matured, He learned to do what He was supposed to do when He was supposed to do it. As Scripture tells us, He spent much time in prayer. (See Matt. 14:23; Mark 1:35; Luke 6:12; 9:18,28; 11:1.)

Children Are Born Undisciplined

The opposite of maturity is immaturity. An immature person has to be watched all the time. He is immature because he has no self-discipline. But a child won't know self-discipline until he has been disciplined by his parent.

Children are born undisciplined. They cry when they want something and when they don't want something, and then they

---

[1] John Walvoord and Roy B. Zuck, *The Bible Knowledge Commentary* (Wheaton, Illinois: Victor, 1983), p. 210.

yell in between. That's why they need Pampers. They must be trained and disciplined.

As cute and cuddly as little kids can be, if left untrained, as they get older they won't be cute and cuddly anymore. Their behavior turns into rebellion, and then everybody gets upset.

Now there is a Bible way to handle discipline. We will be very practical in these chapters on the subject of discipline. As mentioned before, God's people aren't like rats in a maze; we are divinely ordered. We have a destination, with a purpose and a plan, not only as a church but as a family and as individuals.

All of us have a divine plan and a divine call on our lives. But we have to realize that there are some rules to life. It's one thing to get excited about having a vision, but there are rules we have to follow.

That's why a believer could get a ticket for speeding when driving down the highway going 57 miles an hour in a 55 mph zone, while an unbeliever goes 90 miles an hour and never gets caught. As the Bible says, **...judgment must begin at the house of God** (1 Pet. 4:17).

Follow God's Rules

When our family is out in public, I don't discipline other people's children, just my own. I have set a standard for _my_ children, not for the children down the street. I want to do according to Micah 6:8, which says:

He hath shewed thee, O man, what is good; and what doth the Lord require of thee, but _to do justly_, and _to love mercy_, and _to walk humbly with thy God?_

There are three things God requires of His people:

Number one: _to do justly._

Number two: _to love mercy._

Number three: _to walk humbly._

Three Areas We Have to Fight

It seems that the number-one statement of all children every-where is: "But that isn't fair!"

That's why I say to my kids, "That's right, honey — life isn't fair."

The devil is an equal-opportunity hater. He hates everybody the same — whether a little baby, a middle-aged person or just an old grouch.

Now there are three areas we have to fight against on this planet:

1. the world system, which is the opposite of whatever God thinks;

2. the devil, whom we have authority over in the name of Jesus and by His blood; and

3. the flesh, which is the area we are dealing with most of the time, particularly in relationship to people.

The devil works at attacking the home. As we can see in the Bible, he hates the home. That's what he attacked right off the bat when he came against Adam and Eve's family in the beginning, and he has been working against the home ever since. The devil caused Adam to be fired from his job, his family to be evicted from their home and their children to be killing each other. But we don't have to be ignorant of the devil's devices.

Provoke Not Your Children

Ephesians 6:4 is a key Scripture for the second word of our study, *discipline.*

Often we parents have made our children memorize verses 1-3 of this chapter from Ephesians, which says:

Children, obey your parents in the Lord: for this is right.

Honour thy father and mother; which is the first commandment with promise;

That it may be well with thee, and thou mayest live long
on the earth.

We make our children memorize these verses of Scripture, but
then we ourselves avoid the first part of the very next verse, verse
4, which says:

And, ye fathers, provoke not your children to wrath....

We bypass these words by jumping to the second part of this
verse, which says:

...but bring them up in the nurture and admonition of
the Lord.

Now this wording in the _King James Version_ is a little flowery,
so let me offer a further explanation. The Greek word for _nurture_
is _paideia_, which means child discipline, including directing and
correcting and training in righteousness.[2]

There must be rules and regulations which lead to either
rewards or punishment. You reward your children for keeping the
rules, and you punish them when those rules are broken. To
nurture is to train by rules and regulations, backed up by rewards
and punishments.

Faith Is to Be Passed On to Our Children

When I was in a college Bible class on Christian leadership, we
were given a test. There were seventeen young men in that class.
Our professor said: "Gentlemen, I'm going to give you several pairs
of people from the Bible. I want you to pick out which one of the
two you consider to be the best leader." He then gave us six pairs.
All we had to do was go through our Bible, do some research and
choose whom we considered the best leader of each pair.

---

[2] WALVOORD AND ZUCK, _THE BIBLE KNOWLEDGE COMMENTARY_, P. 642.

The first pair given to us was Moses and Joshua. Basically, Moses was a hothead who kept losing his temper. He smote the rock instead of speaking to it, so he wasn't allowed to go into the Promised Land and finish the job he had started. Everybody knows a good leader finishes what he starts, but Moses wasn't able to do that. (See Num. 20:1-12.)

Joshua was the one who finished the job. He took the Promised Land. He marched around the walls of Jericho until they fell. He got the job done. (See Josh. 1:1-9 and ch. 6.)

So, as great as Moses was, we picked Joshua, seeing him as obviously the better leader of the two.

The second pair given to us was Elijah and Elisha. Elijah had some great miracles and did some great things, but he was constantly griping, murmuring and complaining. He wanted to die, but he wouldn't stand still long enough to let Jezebel kill him. He ran for his life! (See 1 Kings 19.)

Then God said to Elijah, "That's it! I have somebody waiting in the wings to take your place, so you're coming home." (Author's paraphrase.) God sent down the fiery chariot and Elijah was taken home to be with the Lord. Elisha took his place, asking for a double portion of Elijah's spirit to come on him, and it did. Elisha did twice the miracles that Elijah had done. (See 2 Kings 2.)

So after reading and studying about these two prophets, we picked Elisha. There was no doubt to us that Elisha was a better leader than Elijah.

When we had finished our research and made our choices, we turned in the results to the professor. After reading our report, he said, "Gentlemen, you've done a good job of research. Your choices are very factual — but very wrong."

Looking at one another, we said, "But we can't be wrong. There's no way. We went through every Scripture."

Then he continued: "Listen to me, gentlemen: The most important thing on this planet is the work of God. The work of

God was going on here before you came; and, if Jesus tarries, the work of God will continue after you are gone.

"When Moses went home to be with the Lord, the work of God continued because he had trained up somebody underneath him named Joshua to continue that work. Yet when Joshua went home to be with the Lord, no successor was left.

"Elijah, though reluctantly, trained up Elisha, because Elisha dogged his heels. He left a successor to continue the work of God, and it flourished. But when Elisha went home to be with the Lord, there was no successor left.

"The most important thing we can do is to pass on our faith to the next generation: our children."

Then It Goes From *Your* Children to *Theirs*

Parenting is a lifelong, lifetime process. It isn't saying to children, "Well, after your first eighteen years, let's test you out and see how you did." There is no test you can give them after their first eighteen years or their first thirty-five years.

As the Bible says in the book of Proverbs:

Proverbs 17:6 — **Children's children are the crown of old men; and the glory of children are their fathers.**

Paraphrased, this verse is saying: "We really won't know what kind of parent we have been until we see our grandchildren. If we put enough of the Word of God into our children's hearts and they pass it on to their kids, then we did our job."

In Genesis 18:19 the Lord said of Abraham:

For I know him, that he will command his children and his household after him (meaning his grandchildren and all his servants), **and they shall keep the way of the Lord, to do justice and judgment; that the Lord may bring upon Abraham that which he hath spoken of him.**

In paraphrasing this verse, God was saying: "I will bring these blessings upon Abraham, for I know he won't become a grumpy old man, hoarding all these blessings to himself. He will teach his children how he came across these blessings and he will pass on to them, not only material things, but a knowledge of Me."

The way I see it, my children will inherit my properties without doing a thing. All I have to do is die; then they will receive all the physical things I have accumulated. But they will never just automatically inherit my knowledge. That has to be earned.

It's my responsibility as a parent to set a table before my children, but they have to eat it for themselves. I have to create an atmosphere conducive for them to want and desire it, and then to eat it. I have to make sure I am not provoking my children to wrath by being unreasonable and unjust and in a bad mood all the time.

Set Up Some Rules

How do we keep from provoking our children to wrath? By setting up some rules and regulations for everyone in the household.

Now for you to have rules and regulations that really work, it's important to remember one point: Don't overdo it. You can't be setting up four hundred rules and regulations. Children won't remember that many. They might remember two — maybe.

As we get further into our study on discipline, I want to remind you — and I would keep reiterating it — that children are children and they do childish things. So you had better allow them to be that way.

If you intend to discipline your kids, make sure you enforce the rules. Don't make a rule if you can't or won't take the time to enforce it.

Don't give idle threats, telling your child, "If you do such-and-such, I'm going to do thus-and-so." Don't make such threats unless you really mean it. You would then be making a mockery out of the whole system, and your kids won't listen to you. That's when they will start talking back.

If I am not going to take the time to enforce a rule, I don't even want to set that rule.

Train Up a Child

A key Scripture right here is Proverbs 22:6, which we quoted earlier in our study. Again, it says:

> Train up a child in the way he should go: and when he is old, he will not depart from it.

Notice it says, **Train up a child in _the way he should go_.**

This verse in _The Amplified Bible_ reads:

> Train up a child in the way he should go [and in keeping with his individual gift or bent], and when he is old he will not depart from it.

In other words, train up a child according to his individual bent. That means each child has a gift or bent, a direction in life to be fulfilled.

Be Flexible

Train up a child in _the way_ he should go. The Hebrew word translated _way_ in this verse is _derek_[3]. Another place this word appears in the Old Testament is in Proverbs 30. This Scripture says:

> Proverbs 30:18,19 — **There be three things which are too wonderful for me, yea, four which I know not:**

---

[3] JAMES H. STRONG. _STRONG'S EXHAUSTIVE CONCORDANCE._ COMPACT ED. (GRAND RAPIDS: BAKER, 1992), "HEBREW AND CHALDEE DICTIONARY," P. 31, #1870.

(1) The way of an eagle in the air; (2) the way of a serpent upon a rock; (3) the way of a ship in the midst of the sea; and (4) the way of a man with a maid.

This Scripture is dealing with flexibility. We will get into point number four later in our study regarding dating and sex, but for right now let's look at the first three areas mentioned here in verse 19:

1. *The way of an eagle in the air.*

An eagle will fly out in the morning looking for food. It isn't like a little sparrow or a hummingbird, which is always fluttering and flapping its wings. When a big gust of wind picks up suddenly, the eagle doesn't panic; it simply keeps its wings spread out. Whatever way the wind is blowing, the eagle just rides up over it and comes down on the other side. The eagle is flexible. It may have to turn and make a few adjustments, but it still gets where it's going.

2. *The way of a serpent upon a rock.*

When I grew up in East Tennessee, I did a lot of trout fishing and spent plenty of time in the mountain streams. During that time, I saw rabbit trails, deer trails and dog trails, but never a snake trail. That's because there is no such thing as a snake trail around those streams.

I have been standing in the middle of many a stream and looked over toward the bank in time to see a copperhead slide out of its nest and into the water. (That's when I left the water!)

I have watched those snakes. They come down across the rocks where the waterfalls are located. If there is a dip in those rocks, they go down in it; if there is a jagged edge, they come up over it.

I never saw one of those snakes get frustrated and say, "Doggone it! There's no rock over here; I have to go down that way!" That snake never griped about the terrain; it just kept rolling along. Whether faced with a high rock or a puddle of water, it moved right through it or around it or over it. But it always got where it was going. It was flexible.

3. *The way of a ship in the midst of the sea.*

When a ship leaves England coming to America, the gyroscope is set in the bell of that ship and it knows where it's going. But sometimes there are currents. Sometimes there are twenty- or thirty-foot waves.

I don't think a sea captain has ever said, "I'm not going over that wave; I'm going right through the middle of it. So that wave had just better get out of my way!"

A ship will never go through the middle of any wave. It has to ride over it and come down on the other side. It has to be flexible.

The same is true with parents and how they handle their kids.

If there is a key word in training your children and making rules and regulations, it is *flexible*. You had better be flexible. The moment you get rigid and legalistic is the moment you are going to reap the whirlwind.

Now I am not talking against having a standard. As I mentioned before, I believe in setting high standards; my children will tell you that. But I am also flexible, and here's why: Psalm 127:3 says, **Lo, children are an heritage of the Lord: and the fruit of the womb is his reward.** Children are a reward from God to us. They are given to us as a reward. It's our job to train them up and give them back to the Lord. He will then use them for His glory.

No Standard

When I was the school administrator, a mom and dad brought their fourteen-year-old son to my office. I had known that family for some time.

When they got into the lobby, I could hear them yelling. Then when they brought the boy into my office, they stood there yelling some more.

Basically, the dad was saying, "This boy is just like his mother, running his mouth all the time. He gives me no respect, and he doesn't hit a lick at nothing!" The mom was saying, "He's just like his dad, sitting around all day watching TV and belching, and he doesn't hit a lick at nothing!"

Pointing at his son, the dad said to me, and I quote: "Mr. McGee, we want you to fix him. We'll be back in a little bit. We're going to the mall." Then they left him there with me.

When the parents had left, I looked at the boy and he looked at me. Obviously, we weren't going anywhere with our conversation, so I bought him a soft drink; then we went outside, walked around the parking lot and talked for an hour.

About an hour-and-a-half later, the dad came back. He seemed to be feeling proud of himself for handling the situation, so he said to me, "Well, tell me what happened."

I guess he thought I would just sprinkle some dust like magic, lay my hands on his boy and cast out a few devils — then everything would be wonderful! But I didn't do any of those things. The boy and I just visited.

So the dad said, "Tell me, Joe, why has my son been acting like an idiot?"

I didn't even have to prepare my response. These words just came out: "Dad, your son has been acting like an idiot because he thinks like an idiot. And he thinks like an idiot because he feeds on idiot stuff. The Bible says, 'As a man thinks in his heart, so is he.'"[4]

Children can be acting strange because they are thinking strange. They think strange because they have been feeding on strange ideas. Whatever goes into their little eyes and ears is what they will think about and then do. It's very simple. Now a psychiatrist would charge you big money for this information, but it's free — from me to you.

---

[4] PROVERBS 23:7.

Spend Time With Your Kids

Again, as Proverbs 22:6 says, **Train up a child in the way he should go: and when he is old, he will not depart from it.**

Now listen carefully. Let's say the average dad spends three minutes per day per child in some sort of meaningful conversation. That would be saying something other than comments like, "Sit down and shut up," "Take out the trash," "Clean up your room," "Do your homework," "Feed the dog." Let's say the average mom spends six minutes per day per child. That would come to a grand total of 2.25 twenty-four-hour days out of 365. Perhaps some parents spend more time, some less.

Let's say your child regularly attends church, going three times a week for at least an hour of instruction every time the doors open, and never misses a Sunday or a Wednesday for fifty-two weeks. If you add up all that time spent in church, it comes to a grand total of approximately 6.5 twenty-four-hour days out of 365.

Since 1852, there has been a compulsory school attendance law in our nation. A child must go to school somewhere — whether public, private or home school — usually for 180 days out of the year. If you add up all of those days, with six hours a day of uninterrupted instruction, that comes to just over 45 twenty-four-hour days out of 365.[5]

In Luke 6:40, quoting from *The Amplified Bible*, Jesus said, **A pupil is not superior to his teacher, but everyone [when he is] completely trained...will be like his teacher.**

A child, when fully taught, will be just like his teacher. The child will start to pick up whatever that teacher values. Now this verse doesn't say the child will know what his teacher knows. That's why a kid can sit in a classroom for nine months and still make an F.

---

[5] D. Bruce Lockerbie, *Who Educates Your Child* (Grand Rapids: Zondervan, 1980), p. 3.

The average American child between the ages of twelve and seventeen consumes just over 28 twenty-four-hour days of television time, *not including* videos, radio, cassettes, CDs, computer games, magazines or comic books.[6] Information given out during media time is written on a sixth-grade level and appeals to nothing but the carnal nature.

Now if our kids are consuming 28 days of television time (not including all the other forms of media), spending 45 days in school and 6 days in church and 2.25 days communicating with Mom and Dad, is it any wonder that kids act the way they do?

As for our kids, we haven't done righteously. Let me tell you, humanism is a good buzz word being used these days. Humanists are just people trying to help our families, but they don't know God. They are ever learning but aren't able to come to the knowledge of the truth. They see what we Christians do as crazy, ineffective and religious brainwashing.

Childproofing the Home

Parents have usually come to me for counseling because they had what they called a "discipline problem."

One mother said, "Mr. McGee, I spanked my toddler fifteen times yesterday." (I don't know if she really did it, but that's what she said.) I could see the frustration in her.

I said, "Mom, that's about fourteen too many. What's the problem?"

Then she started rattling off: "Well, the kid ate the dog food and the plants. He pulled out all the silverware and got into my pots and pans. Then he took something out of my billfold and flushed it down the toilet; it disappeared just as I got there, and I don't know what it was!"

---

[6] *THE 1995 WORLD ALMANAC:*
FUNK AND WAGNALLS, 1994, P. 310.

She wanted to know what she should do with her rebellious toddler.

I said: "Hold it, Mama. You don't have a rebellion problem; you have an ignorance problem. Number one, the dog food should go outside with the dog. Number two, get rid of those real plants and keep plastic plants around the house until your child gets a little older. Number three, go to the hardware store and buy locks to fasten up all the drawers. And number four, put your billfold and pocketbook in the top of the closet out of your kid's reach. If you're going to have kids, you need to childproof your home."

A child's playtime is the same as our work time, and children are very diligent workers. When preschoolers and toddlers wake up in the morning, it's as if they are punching a clock. You may think they are just making messes, but they are working. They work all day long at what appears to be destroying property. They can do things like chew the corners off end tables or paint on the walls. They don't have to take lunch breaks or nap breaks; they just work constantly.

When kids get through with the day, they look back at all they have done and feel so proud of themselves. Then at night they don't have to work at going to sleep; they just pass out. Mom or Dad has to pick up their limp little bodies, put them in bed and cover them up.

I remember reading a story one time about the cruise ship, Queen Mary, being pulled into dock to be made into a hotel. The smokestacks were to be taken down and reworked. But when a large crane was hooked to the smokestacks to lift them off the deck of the ship, they just exploded into dust. Nothing was left but that swinging crane. Engineers were brought in to find out what had happened, and as it turned out, there were no smokestacks, only about one hundred twenty coats of epoxy paint. Those smokestacks had just rusted away years ago.

It wouldn't surprise me that, many years from now, maybe during the Millennium, if you went to my house, there wouldn't be any house left; everything would have gone back to the dust.

But no doubt you would be able to see where all of the walls had been. Still standing would be about one hundred twenty coats of paint! That's because my kids have worked on a continual basis at autographing the walls of our home. That's just the kind of thing children do.

Children Are Like Arrows

Psalm 127:4,5 — **As arrows are in the hand of a mighty man; so are children of the youth.**

Happy is the man that hath his quiver full of them: they shall not be ashamed, but they shall speak with the enemies in the gate.

Now let me tell you a little story about arrows being used in Jewish warfare. We find the Israelites going into battle one day with their quivers full of arrows.

Now people always ask, "How many are in a quiver?" Some say seven; some say twenty-four. I don't know how many there were, but you need to seek God about how many you want in your quiver!

In those days, soldiers didn't buy their arrows at Wal-Mart or Kmart or the sporting goods store. Those arrows didn't come two dozen to a box with all of them being the same length and the same size; they had to be individually cut from a tree. Can you picture some guy shinning up a tree and cutting off branches to be used in making arrows? That's why no two arrows were ever the same!

Let's imagine what it was like one day when the Israelites were battling against one of their archenemies. An Israeli soldier was standing there, shooting his arrows at the enemy, when all of a sudden he saw this big ugly guy coming at him. The guy was holding one knife in each hand and another between his teeth.

Looking at his enemy, the Israelite said to himself, *He's coming after me! This isn't good!* So he reached into his quiver for an arrow.

But he wasn't looking for just any arrow; he was looking for the biggest, fattest arrow he had ever cut. When he found it, he pulled it from the quiver and set it in his bow. Then he drew it back, aimed it toward that big guy, shot it off and dropped him dead!

When that was done, he thought the battle was over. But then he looked out across the field and saw one fleeing enemy soldier with long, lanky legs. Looking down at his own short legs, he thought, *This will never work. If that guy gets away, he will tell the other ten thousand enemy soldiers where I am.* He could feel panic rising up inside himself.

Then he thought, *I need another arrow,* so again he reached back in his quiver. But this time he was looking for the longest, skinniest arrow that he had. When he found it, he pulled it out, put it in his bow and shot it away. *Ssssspptt! Boom!* That arrow flew out about three hundred yards and dropped the enemy dead. Then the battle was over, and everybody was happy!

All the other soldiers went back to camp for some chow, while he stayed to pick up the spoils of war, but that didn't bother him a bit. As he worked, he sang praises to his Jehovah God about how good God was.

As the sun was going down behind the mountain, he had a load of loot packed on his back and was carrying more under his arms and in his pockets. Walking up the path, he saw movement at the top of a rock, and he knew he had a problem: an enemy soldier was hiding behind that rock!

In a flash he dropped all those spoils of war. At that moment it was as if there was no Jehovah God, as if his God had just moved off to some other planet. (That's how it can be sometimes when we are faced with a trial; we can just temporarily forget about God.)

Then panic struck. He thought, *What am I going to do? If I don't get out of here before the sun goes down, I'll be dog meat in the morning!*

So he reached back in his quiver to see if there were any arrows left. Thank God...one arrow! Then he pulled it out. But when he saw it, his heart sank to his ankles. It was that good-for-nothing, won't-amount-to-a-hill-of-beans kind of arrow. Every time he had shot one of those arrows, it had hooked away from the target. The only reason he had kept it was because, if necessary, he could use it as a weapon to stab an enemy to death.

Realizing his predicament, he started crying out to God, "God, I'm going to die! Help!"

Then God said, "Put that arrow in the bow."

"But, God, it's no good. It's a bad arrow. It's never going to be good for anything!"

"I said for you to put the arrow in the bow!"

"Okay, God, I'll put it in the bow."

Then God said, "Now aim it away from the target, pull it back and let it go."

So in obedience he shot it away, and that arrow hooked like a boomerang around the target. *Ssssspptt! Boom!* The enemy behind that rock dropped dead!

You see, our children are like those arrows. Every arrow is different. Each one will react and respond differently. But they all have a divine purpose. The same basic laws are used for all of them. But as a parent we have to be a little flexible.

5

A Child's Respect for Authority

Our children are going to face temptations, tests and trials. That's just a part of life.

The Bible doesn't say they will be immune from such experiences. It does say, however, that they can go through the water and it won't overtake them, and through the fire and they won't be burned. (Isa. 43:2.) They can come out on the other side and be overcomers.

They will be faced with certain situations that try to lead them off in some other direction, away from God. But with God's Word hidden in their heart, God can begin dealing with them about it. When they hear a nudge from Him, His Spirit will be speaking to their heart. But at the same time, the devil will be tempting them through their thoughts or their flesh. (Every day our children are faced with decisions to do both good and bad.) Each time your child needs to make a decision, there is a three-member board meeting going on inside him.

Spirit, Soul, Body

To understand the makeup of every human being, picture a target drawn on a piece of paper with three circles, one inside the other. Each circle represents a portion of man's nature: spirit, soul and body. The smallest circle in the center is like a bull's-eye, and it represents our human spirit. It's surrounded by a larger circle, which represents our soul (the mind, will and emotions).

Then that circle is surrounded by an even larger circle, representing our physical body.

In every situation a child's spirit will be saying yes to God while his flesh is saying no to Him. *Every* time — without exception! The devil will be tempting him by having somebody or something trying to entice him and lead him away to do wrong. His flesh will respond by saying, "Go ahead and do it!" But his spirit will be saying, "No way! I'm not doing that! Just forget it!" In every situation like this, there will be a tie vote between his flesh and his spirit. That's when his soul will have to break the tie by choosing sides.

First Thessalonians 5:23 refers to our beings as "spirit," "soul" and "body":

> **And the very God of peace sanctify you wholly; and I pray God your whole spirit and soul and body be preserved blameless unto the coming of our Lord Jesus Christ.**

Now I want to give you three Scriptures for the words, *spirit, soul* and *body*.

For *spirit*, Second Corinthians 5:17 says:

> **Therefore if any man be in Christ, he is a new creature: old things are passed away; behold, all things are become new.**

When we accept Jesus Christ as our Lord and Savior, we are born again — taken from the kingdom of darkness and placed into the kingdom of God. Our human spirit becomes a new creature in Christ.

For *soul*, Romans 12:2 says:

> **And be not conformed to this world: but be ye transformed by the *renewing of your mind*, that ye may prove what is that good, and acceptable, and perfect, will of God.**

For *body*, Romans 8:23 says:

...even we ourselves groan within ourselves, waiting for the adoption, to wit, the *redemption of our body.*

As an example, let's say we have a seven-year-old boy named Johnny, who has just been saved by receiving Jesus as the Lord of his life. He has become a new creature in Christ. He knows his name is written in the Lamb's Book of Life, and he is looking forward to heaven. He has just started reading his Bible and finding out how he is to be growing up in the grace and knowledge of his Lord Jesus Christ.

According to Scripture, Johnny should be busy every day renewing his mind (or his soul) with the Word of God.

The physical body Johnny lives in here on earth has no good thing in it. At death, it will go back to the dust. So Johnny's flesh will fight against his spirit. If allowed, he would be eating candy until he made himself sick and watching TV until his eyeballs fell out on the carpet. His flesh wants constantly to be sitting on the throne over his inner man — his spirit.

Johnny's spirit will always go with God, but his flesh never will; his spirit will never go with the devil, but his flesh always will. So, whether God is leading him or the devil is tempting him, there will always be a tie vote.

Who is left to cast the deciding vote? The soul, that's who. (Gal. 5:17.) That's why God says in Hosea 4:6, *My* **people are destroyed for lack of knowledge.**

Our Soul Casts the Deciding Vote

Now the part of our person that will influence what goes on with every situation we face is not our spirit or our flesh but our soul.

The degree to which our children have the Word of God in them is the degree to which they will make wise decisions in their lives when needed. If they don't know the Word of God, they will be incapable of making wise decisions and their flesh will win out every time. That's why the Bible says:

Colossians 3:16 — **Let the word of Christ dwell in you richly....**

The Spirit of God will bring to our remembrance all of the words Jesus spoke. How do we get the words Jesus spoke into our child's heart? As Isaiah 28:10 says, it will be **...precept upon precept; line upon line...here a little, and there a little.** It's giving our child one bite at a time, with lots of repetition.

In Deuteronomy 6:6,7 God said:

And these words, which I command thee this day, shall be in thine heart:

And thou shalt teach them diligently unto thy children, and shalt talk of them when thou sittest in thine house, and when thou walkest by the way, and when thou liest down, and when thou risest up.

This means we are to be teaching our children the truths of God's Word when we wake up in the morning, when we walk throughout the day, when we sit down and when we lie down. We are to be a constant reminder to them of God's ways and purposes in this life.

In America, parents seem to be trying to train up their children by always giving them "things." They want their children to have a certain kind of education and to wear a certain kind of clothing. Then after providing their children with all those "things," the parents wonder why their children don't turn out right.

But their children have never been given God's Word. With no Word, they will have no wisdom. They need wisdom to have a long life and honor and riches here on earth.

The most important thing we can ever do as a parent is to see to it that we plant the Word of God in our child's heart.

Flesh Pulls On Us Like Gravity

One time we were on a trip flying from Abilene, Texas, to Dallas, Texas. That journey was an interesting one, to say the least. When we left Abilene, we were on a fourteen-passenger airliner. That little plane had some screws missing from its inner side; it was shaking and rattling, and lots of black smoke was coming from its engines. All of us on board were wondering how far we would get, just hoping and praying we would make it all the way to Dallas.

After we landed in Dallas and connected with our next flight, we transferred to a much larger airliner. It was like a floating battleship, a massive piece of machinery. It was like we had gone from hell to heaven in one day!

It's hard to imagine how anything as large as that chunk of metal could ever make it off the ground. But there are some physical laws involved. The law of gravity had that plane plastered to the concrete there at the airport. But when the pilot turned on the engines, the law of thrust came into play, forcing that big chunk of metal to move out from the ramp and onto the runway. Then the power of those engines caused that plane to pick up speed. The law of lift, joining with the law of thrust, allowed the plane to leave the runway and overcome the law of gravity.

Now read this carefully: The law of gravity is like our flesh, always wanting to hold us down. The law of thrust is like our spirit, always wanting to get us on the move. According to Romans 8:14, as sons and daughters of God, we are led by the Spirit of God. That means we are going somewhere. We are on the move.

But the pilot could be running that airplane all around the airport. He could be going two hundred miles an hour and never involve the law of lift (knowledge of God's Word). He could be moving without ever leaving the ground. The law of thrust and the law of gravity would be canceling out each other all day long.

Lots of Christians are just like that. They have no real knowledge of God's Word. They have been born again, maybe even

Spirit filled, with their names written in the Lamb's Book of Life. They are staying busy for God, saying: "Praise His holy name! I just hope I can make it to the end, and I hope God helps me sometimes. He ought to be helping me — I'm helping Him."

These believers are running and burning for God, just like that big airplane was running all around the airport. But is the guy behind the controls ever going to get it off the ground?

To do that though, the pilot must have some knowledge. He can pull back that little lever without ever getting off the ground. That's why pilots go to school: to get some knowledge about how to force that big chunk of metal to leave the ground. Once he has the knowledge, he can apply the law of lift with the law of thrust. As a result, the law of gravity will be canceled out and that big chunk of metal will just ease up into the air like a bird.

But when that happens, the law of gravity isn't eliminated; it still exists. The moment the law of lift and the law of thrust cease working together, that big chunk of metal will drop to the ground like a rock!

The same thing will happen in our lives and in our children's lives if there is no Word at work in us. As the Bible says, sin is crouched at the door and waiting. (See Gen. 4:7 AMP.) Our flesh will alienate us if we give it half a chance. As Jesus said, **The spirit indeed is willing, but the flesh is weak** (Matt. 26:41).

We have to be renewing our mind with the Word of God, growing in the knowledge and grace of God.

As I said before, the degree to which our children know the Word of God is the degree to which they will make wise decisions. When the Word and the spirit are in agreement, the flesh will be canceled out. But it is futile to simply try to get our child's flesh to obey without at the same time teaching him to hide God's Word in his heart.

That's why our children need to be involved in church, whether it be Sunday school, vacation Bible school, a Bible study or a youth group. They need to be getting the Word of God into their spirits.

Taking Time To Give a Word to Our Children

As a parent we must get up in the morning and be the number-one cheerleader for our children by giving them some Scripture. I don't mean you need to have a Bible study; it only takes thirty seconds to do this. Speak the Word of God to them, saying something like: "Remember, my child, you are the head and not the tail; you are above and not beneath. I believe that everything you set your hand to today is going to prosper."

Now when you do that, your children may just roll their eyes at you. They may be thinking, *There goes Dad — doing that religious thing again.* But you go ahead and do it anyway. The Bible says God watches over His Word to perform it. (Jer. 1:12 AMP.) God isn't watching over *your* word to perform it, but over *His* Word.

Your child may say, "Sure, Dad. Right. Big deal. But, you know, I do have this chemistry test today."

Then you can say, "Well, honey, that's why the Bible says you should study to show yourself approved unto God, a workman that need not be ashamed, but rightly dividing the word of truth."[1]

Ignorance is a terrible thing. The Bible says, **My people are destroyed for lack of knowledge** (Hos. 4:6).

As a parent, you must sow that seed in your child. Just remember that with seed it takes time. When you sow a seed one day, it probably won't come up that same day; but it *will* come up. Just make sure you keep sowing the Word.

Parents Are Trying To Do Right

After a child is born, the first word he learns is *no*. Where did he learn it? From his parents. About two hundred times each day, he hears: "No! Don't do that! Don't touch that!" It seems we spend most of our time either criticizing, correcting or controlling.

---

[1] 2 TIMOTHY 2:15.

Around the house, parents are always warning their child. Dad says, "Don't put your finger in that outlet — it will bite you!" Mommy says, "Don't touch that iron — it's hot!" There is no problem until the moment those parents turn their backs on that child.

When young parents are walking out of church on Sunday morning, it seems the little toddlers are running and the moms keep yelling out, "Don't run!" Those little ones can be told not to run, but all of them are running. They start right away doing the opposite of what they have been told.

Do you know why kids do the opposite? Because those precious little babies were born with a sin nature. It's that sin nature which gives them the inclination to do wrong and always be saying, "Don't you tell me what to do!" The sin nature in all of us says that. It may seem cute when kids are only two years old, but it's rebellion when they get to be twelve.

I see this everywhere I go across the country. Moms and dads are trying to do right. They are ever learning but never able to come into the knowledge of the truth.

Maybe your kid is growing up, but as a two-year-old he still has to be restrained sometimes.

One day while in the grocery store I saw a mother pushing a cart with her little kid riding in the bottom of it. She was going down the aisle where the ketchup, mayonnaise and pickles were located. Her little boy had his hand stuck out and was pushing jars of pickles off the shelf one at a time. _Boom! Boom!_

When I came around the corner, there must have been five or six jars already broken. Vinegar was running all over the floor.

I don't know what was holding that mom's attention, but she hadn't even noticed it yet. Then all of a sudden she looked down and saw what had happened. She must have chased that kid all around the store, finally catching him over in the bread section.

Another time we were in Wal-Mart. Being summer, it was hot, miserable and sticky. The temperature must have been about 104 degrees. Mothers were out shopping that day, not because it was the leisurely thing to do, but because it was a necessity.

While at the check-out counter, I noticed a mother standing there with her child. Her cart was full of merchandise. The child, holding bubblegum in one hand and candy in the other, was pulling on her, saying, "Mama? Mama?" She wasn't responding, just standing there and staring off into space.

All of a sudden she turned around, lunged toward the kid and did a belly flop on her cart. Then she jumped up and chased him out into the lobby. Everyone heard it when she caught him. *Slap! Slap! Slap!* When she walked back inside, the child wasn't with her. She came over to the cashier, wrote out a check for the merchandise and walked out.

In this country parents are trying to do what is right. They say, "Well, we heard that we need to make our children obey." That's right; we do. We sometimes have to apply external control over our child's flesh.

Setting External Controls

There are two stages of growth that our children go through, which we have to deal with as parents: from newborn to about twelve years of age and from about thirteen years to maturity. Let's consider each of these.

Newborn to Twelve

From newborn to twelve is what we call the training time. That's when the parent says, "Jump," and the child asks, "How high?"

Our kids must be trained to say, "Yes, sir," "No, sir," "Yes, ma'am," "No, ma'am." They must be taught, "Do this" and "Don't do that."

As a parent, I am the most powerful influence in my children's lives until they are about twelve. I tell them everything: when to get up, when to go to bed, what to wear, what to eat, where to go, who their friends will be and what they can watch on TV. I am their brain. Now this may sound harsh, but it isn't really as severe as it sounds.

Sometimes even before the age of twelve, depending on the child, we can start to release some responsibilities, saying to our children words like: "You're old enough to make some minor decisions on your own. I realize you might bite the dust a little bit, but that's okay. You'll learn from it."

Thirteen to Maturity

Thirteen to maturity is when the parents have to answer their children's big question, "Why?"

Children can ask their parents questions like, "Mom, is it important that we believe in the Virgin Birth?" or "Dad, is it important that we be filled with the Holy Spirit and pray in the Spirit?"

Your children will start asking questions that will make you study. Maybe you don't know why you have been believing certain things. Maybe you just believe that way because your parents believed it. You may say to your child, "That's just the way we believe, so you had better believe that way too." But that won't work! You have to start teaching your kids about things based on God's Word.

Around the age of thirteen is when children turn into that subculture called teenagers.

It's during this time that what looked and sounded so cute from your child of age two seems more like outright rebellion when he becomes a teenager. He just looks you in the face and says, "I'm not doing that anymore — and you can't make me!"

That's when you ask yourself, *What happened?* You thought you had done all you were supposed to do by putting the external control on your child. That worked as long as you were bigger than him; you could yell at him and whip him if he got out of line. But now, all of a sudden, he is as big as you are and can look you eyeball to eyeball. He knows he could perhaps whip you if he wanted to.

Our Children Must Be Taught a Little at a Time

The problem is, parents miss something very important. So many of them sit in my office, saying, "We did everything the Bible said for us to do."

"Exactly what did you do?" I ask.

"Well, we disciplined when we were supposed to and we had our kids in church all the time."

But you need to realize that just having your kids in church is no automatic answer.

There are some laws that have to hook up together. Let's look at Isaiah 28:9,10. It says:

> **Whom shall he teach knowledge? and whom shall he make to understand doctrine? them that are weaned from the milk, and drawn from the breasts.**
>
> **For precept must be upon precept, precept upon precept; line upon line, line upon line; here a little, and there a little.**

If we have been doing according to this Scripture and putting the Word of God into our child's heart, by the time he is twelve we will no longer need external controls because internal controls have been set within him.

Then the Spirit of God will bring conviction to the Word that has been placed within our children. They won't do something now just because Mom and Dad said so. They will do it because God is convicting them and they know it's the right thing to do.

A Parent's Failure

Let's look in the Old Testament at the story of Eli. Here Eli, who was in full-time ministry, had two sons, Hophni and Phinehas. God was trying to deal with Eli. Speaking to the prophet Samuel, God says:

1 Samuel 3:12,13 — **In that day I will perform against Eli all things which I have spoken concerning his house: when I begin, I will also make an end.**

For I have told him that I will judge his house for ever for the iniquity which he knoweth; because his sons made themselves vile, and he restrained them not.

God was not saying for Eli to go and talk to his sons, but to restrain them. God was telling him, "Eli, you need to make your sons stop doing what they are doing. They are committing vile acts at the temple gates, so do something about it."

We know of three times that God had tried to warn the prophet Samuel. After hearing it from God directly, Samuel in turn shared the message with Eli. God was telling Eli to restrain his sons, but Eli wouldn't do it.

Finally, it was as if God said, "That's it. I'm not putting up with it anymore."

Then the Philistines came against Israel. Scripture says:

1 Samuel 4:10,11 — **And the Philistines fought, and Israel was smitten, and they fled every man into his tent: and there was a very great slaughter; for there fell of Israel thirty thousand footmen.**

And the ark of God was taken; and the two sons of Eli, Hophni and Phinehas, were slain.

A runner came and told Eli what had happened; and, as a result, verse 18 tells how Eli fell backward off his stool, broke his neck and died.

The Prophet's Failure as a Parent

Growing up in Eli's house, Samuel saw all of this happen. Then Samuel went on to be the greatest judge and prophet that Israel had seen to that point. On several occasions he interceded on behalf of the nation and God moved mightily through his life.

But do you know what happened when Samuel grew old? It seems that Samuel's own two boys turned out to be worse than Eli's. Scripture says:

1 Samuel 8:1,3-5 — **And it came to pass, when Samuel was old, that he made his sons judges over Israel....**

And his sons walked not in his ways, but turned aside after lucre, and took bribes, and perverted judgment.

Then all the elders of Israel gathered themselves together, and came to Samuel unto Ramah,

And said unto him, Behold, thou art old, and thy sons walk not in thy ways: now make us a king to judge us like all the nations.

The Israelites were saying to Samuel, "You're getting old and are about to die, and we don't want those two ratty, rebellious sons of yours ruling over us. We want a king." But it wasn't the will of God for Israel to have a king.

That's why we as parents can go to church all day long and have miracles happening in our lives, and still see our children heading straight for hell.

Listen to me carefully: The way our children get saved is by being led to the saving knowledge of Jesus. Now it's going to take some prayer over them and the sowing of God's Word into their lives, with our living a life for them to model, but they will be saved. There are several factors involved.

Now you may be saying, "Well, I love the Lord and I've been going to church all my life, so my children will too, and I just know they're going to grow up to serve Him."

But children won't just love God automatically. As the Bible says, we have to train them up in the way they should go. (Prov. 22:6.)

What have you been telling your children about God? Have you been living upright before them?

Children don't just do what we say; they do what we do.

Here we see Samuel's reaction to the people's request for a king:

1 Samuel 8:6,7 — But the thing displeased Samuel, when they said, Give us a king to judge us. And Samuel prayed unto the Lord.

And the Lord said unto Samuel, Hearken unto the voice of the people in all that they say unto thee: for they have not rejected thee, but they have rejected me, that I should not reign over them.

Samuel tried to talk the people out of having a king by describing to them the demands that would be made as a result. He was saying: "When you have a king to reign over you, you must build him a house. Then he must be provided with chariots, horsemen and soldiers for war. In support of him, you must give your sons and daughters to work for him, as well as a portion of your lands, your seed and your sheep." (Author's paraphrase; see vv. 10-18.)

But the people still had to have their king, and things just went downhill from there. Why? Because a father wouldn't restrain his children and failed to raise his children right. You don't just tell children what to do. Training means showing them over and over and seeing to it that they do it.

No Respect for Authority

The reason I mention this story from God's Word is because today things are not like they were even five years ago. There is a difference. Child abuse is running rampant in our country and children are being beaten to death every day. Why? Mostly because people don't know how to deal with life, and they get frustrated and angry and upset. This is proof of how much they need the saving grace of the Lord Jesus Christ.

These days the dark is getting darker while the light is getting brighter. Sin is abounding on this earth, but that's great news! For as the Bible says, where sin abounds, grace does much more abound. (Rom. 5:20.) I don't care how high the devil may stick up his head; God's head will always be much higher!

There is an important point having to do with discipline which we must teach our children: They must have respect for authority. There will be people who misuse them, abuse them and say all manner of evil against them, but our children must be strong in spite of all that. Later in this book, we will deal with what the Bible says about getting along with both our friends and our enemies.

Maybe the teacher wasn't fair in the way he acted toward your child. But you can't be allowing your kid to stand up in class and challenge that adult teacher in front of others. That's wrong. If you let that happen, you will lose before you ever get started.

We parents have to teach our children how to respond to authority. There is a right way to make an appeal.

First Timothy 5:1 tells of not rebuking an elder harshly but speaking to him (or her) as you would your father (or mother). It is not wise to let your child stand up in class and call the teacher a knothead.

Matthew 18:15-17 says you make an appeal by going one on one with someone rather than by confronting him in public. If he won't listen to you, take a witness with you and go to him again. If he still won't listen, tell it to the church.

There are certain rules and regulations our children must learn to follow at home.

As I tell children:

"If you don't learn to obey at home, your next step will be refusing to obey at school. By not obeying at school, you will face punishments. First, you may be assigned a lot of written work; then you get grounded from the basketball team, then suspended from school, then expelled. Next, you can get put into juvenile hall, then the county jail, then prison, and eventually the maximum-security prison, perhaps even facing the absolute penalty of death in the electric chair.

"It's a progressive stage, and it gets worse, not better. The sooner you learn to respond to authority, the better life you will have on this planet. You have to know how to respond to authority, because God set up authorities."

According to Romans 13:1-3 NIV, there is no authority except that which God has established and those who rebel against the authority are rebelling against God. It says rulers are not a terror to those who do right but to those who do wrong. You do what is right, and the authority will commend you.

A Shift of Guilt

Your kid may be challenging you and your rules, saying, "But it isn't fair!" That's a shift of guilt. Your child will never repent as long as he can succeed in shifting that guilt in some other direction.

Don't let your child always be saying, "Well, it's So-and-so's fault," or "It's the teacher's fault," or "It's the school's fault." Again, that's a shift of guilt.

By allowing this to happen, you will never see your child repent. A person will only repent when he truly feels remorse.

Shifting the Blame or Repenting

Your child may be saying, "I've done something wrong and I have to get it off my chest." The only way for him to do this would be either by shifting the blame to someone or something else or by repenting.

As long as he can shift the blame in another direction, he will never repent. Instead, he will say something like: "It wasn't *my* fault; it was *Billy's* fault. *He's* the one responsible."

If your child doesn't repent, he will never walk in God's favor and have the blessings of God. You have to get to the place where your child can understand this truth. If you don't, he will never know how to repent and he will be living in bondage to that sin. The only way any of us can get sin out of our life is by repenting of it and confessing it with our mouth.

It seems today that self-esteem seminars are being presented everywhere, in churches as well as in the business world. You can find notices for these self-esteem seminars on street corners in every major city in this country. Why? Because people throughout our country are feeling bad about themselves. The devil is doing his job well.

One person may say, "I'm going to that self-esteem seminar." When asked why, he says: "Because I feel just rotten about myself. The problem must have stemmed from my mother or my father. It has to come from somebody."

I would say to that person, "No, *you're* the problem! Why don't you repent and get that sin out of your life? Then you can start living a good life by the power of God's Holy Spirit at work in you."

For the most part, people have never been confronted. Children have grown up in this society being told things like: "It's not your fault; it's your teacher's fault," or "It's your daddy's fault for going off and leaving us," or "It's your mama's fault for doing wrong."

You know, one of the major methods of controlling children in the classroom today is called behavior modification. This involves getting the child to do something you want without letting him know what you are doing. That is nothing more than manipulation.

Jesus was a confronter. He didn't mess around when it came to sin. He was not out to condemn the world but to convict people of their sin and to lead them to repentance. It is the devil who *condemns*; it is the Lord Jesus Who *convicts*. There is a big difference in these two words.

No, parent, it's *our* fault! If we really love our children, we will repent, which means we will turn and go the other way. As Scripture says, **...the goodness of God leadeth thee to repentance** (Rom. 2:4).

Our children are just looking for somebody with authority; they aren't looking for perfect parents. They are saying to themselves, *Will somebody please show me the right way?*

The Goodness of God

Now that leads me to another Bible story. In Luke's gospel, we find the story of Simon Peter, the fisherman. Peter had been fishing all night long and hadn't caught even one fish. Fish meant money to him, but he hadn't made any money the night before.

The following morning he and his business partners were cleaning their nets on the shore when Jesus stopped by and began speaking to the people. Everybody was crowding in to hear Him until He was almost backed into the water, so He asked Peter if He could borrow his boat. Then Jesus stood on the end of the boat and preached to the crowd.

When His sermon was over and the people had gone home, Jesus turned to Peter and said, "Let's go fishing."

Peter's response might have gone something like this:

"Lord, I know You're a good carpenter. I've bought several pieces of Your furniture; my mother even has some of it in her house. We really like it and I recommend it everywhere I go. Now I know You've ministered to a bunch of people today, Lord, and I'm impressed with what You've said and done. But, Lord, let's face it — You don't know anything about fishing.

"I'm the best fisherman there is, and we've been fishing all night long. We went to all the best places, and there aren't any fish out there. The sun is up now, and we can't catch fish in the daytime. That isn't the kind of fishing we do."

But Jesus said to Peter, "I want you to take out your boat and let down your nets for a catch." (Luke 5:4.)

So Peter said, "Okay, Lord. For You, we'll go out." I think Peter was just giving the Lord lip service, but he had Jesus sit down in the boat.

Evidently, Peter's buddies didn't go out with them. He probably said, "You guys stay here and finish your work. I'm taking the Lord out fishing."

If you read this account in chapter 5 of Luke's gospel, you will see that Jesus said to Peter, **Launch out into the deep, and let down your** *nets* (v. 4). Notice He said *nets* — plural. To show you Peter's half-hearted effort, verse 5 says he let down a *net* — singular. So Peter's attitude was all wrong.

But when he dropped the net (singular), things suddenly began to happen. That net filled up and began to break, then the boat began to sink. Peter forgot all about the Lord. He wasn't consumed with a wonderful, religious *King James* miracle. For him, this meant cash — it was payday!

He started hollering back to shore for help from his partners. "Come quick!" he yelled out. "We're losing it!" Then they all brought out their boat. Everybody was throwing out their nets and pulling them back in, full of fish.

Peter was probably thinking, *Fish! Cash! I have the market cornered now!*

But on the way back to shore, something happened. Peter looked around and saw Jesus there at the end of the boat. The Bible says Peter fell down before Him and said these guilt-ridden words: **Depart from me; for I am a sinful man, O Lord** (v. 8).

Do you know what had just hit Peter? An awareness of the goodness of God. He recognized what God had done for him and he was overwhelmed. He didn't feel worthy of what Jesus had done and he couldn't stand it.

It wasn't a lightning bolt from heaven that got onto him because he wouldn't believe God. It wasn't God Who had some monster come up and bite off his head. But that's how some people view God.

An Excuse for Child Abuse

I remember some "Christian" films we rented for the children to watch at our vacation Bible school. We had about twenty of them, but after seeing only three, that's all we could take.

One of them was the story of a little kid living in Jamaica. He didn't want to go to Sunday school, so he ran away. He got in a canoe and was paddling toward another island. He planned to hide out there and catch fish every day. *After all*, he thought, *I'm a big boy now and I don't have to go to church if I don't want to*. But then the canoe tipped over, and a big shark came at him. *Chop!* It bit off his leg and mangled him really bad.

The end of the film showed the little boy lying there in bed. His leg was gone, and he was bandaged up, with his arm in a sling. But there in front of him laid a Bible. The film was showing how God did all those bad things to bring the boy back home to Him.

Between that and "an act of God," who would want to go to heaven? That film even made hell look kind of good.

Think about it: If God would do that to a little boy, why shouldn't a parent be allowed to beat up on his kid to teach him a thing or two?

Now it's a fact that child abuse is running rampant these days as people are beating up their kids. I see it everywhere I go.

One man who had served as juvenile judge for thirteen years once said to me: "Joe, since I have been on the bench, some of the worst child abusers I have ever seen are born-again Christians who are literally 'beating hell' out of their kids in the name of the Lord."

But a parent's authority doesn't mean this. Let's look now at the subject of discipline in the home.

6

Discipline in the Home

Let me start here with this statement of fact: Discipline without a relationship will breed rebellion in a child. A parent can't be walking around acting like Atilla the Hun or some five-star general, who barks out a few orders and then disappears. That isn't Biblical parenting.

You can talk to your child until you have turned forty shades of blue, but he won't do what he hears you *say*; he does only what he sees you *do*.

I have come to realize that the thing I hate the most in my children is the very thing I find myself guilty of the most.

After watching my children pull some particular stunt, I will ask my wife, "Where did they learn to do that?"

Denise turns to me in surprise and says, "Go look in the mirror."

"I don't do that," I say.

"You're doing it right now," she says.

It seems I can get very animated when I talk, so my children get animated when they talk to me — sometimes too much.

Don't Isolate Your Kids

Isolation is the worst punishment a parent could ever give his child.

Don't ever get mad at your kid and yell out: "Go to your room right now and stay there! You're not getting any supper! You can just stay there till hell freezes over!"

When you act like that, I promise you, every demon in hell is just camped out in your child's bedroom and will be whispering to him what a scumbag you are. As Proverbs 29:15 says, **...a child left to himself bringeth his mother to shame.**

God doesn't isolate His children, and you should never isolate yours. What you have to do is confront the situation, deal with it and get it past you. Isolation is the last form of church discipline. (Matt. 18:17.)

Kids Should Fear the Rod, Not the Parents

Now regarding discipline, if you as a parent don't have control in your home, you can forget about everything else. But being in control doesn't mean beating up your kids.

The child should never fear the parent. He is supposed to fear the rod, so his parent has to teach him that. Let's talk now about the use of the rod.

There is a Bible way to use the rod and a Bible time for correction. The parent must learn when and how it is to be used, and how often.

Before anyone gets a wild idea about misusing the rod, let me make a statement right here: Parents, you must never use the rod on your child for doing anything other than that which he has specifically and repeatedly been told not to do. If you can't follow this rule, you should never touch the rod.

Don't ever use the rod on your kids because they spilled milk at the table or even knocked out the plate-glass window with a baseball. When was the last time you did something careless?

Remember, when making rules and regulations for your household, it's the goodness of God that leads to repentance, so be flexible. (See Rom. 2:4.)

There are two words in the Bible we need to consider regarding discipline: *chastisement,* which is the use of the rod, and *punishment,* which is a child's payback for doing something wrong.

Chastisement

Let's look at what the Scriptures say about the use of the rod. There are eighteen Scriptures on this particular subject. I won't give you all eighteen of them, but I highly recommend that you get a concordance and look up all the verses in the book of Proverbs having to do with this subject.

Proverbs 13:24 — **He that spareth his rod hateth his son: but he that loveth him chasteneth him betimes.**

The word *betimes* comes from the Hebrew word *schâchar,* which means "to be up at a task early."[1] If you love your children, you will chasten them early in life to prevent the long-range disaster of an undisciplined life.

Proverbs 15:10 — **Correction is grievous unto him that forsaketh the way: and he that hateth reproof shall die.**

Proverbs 19:18 — **Chasten thy son while there is hope, and let not thy soul spare for his crying.**

Proverbs 20:30 — **The blueness of a wound cleanseth away evil: so do stripes the inward parts of the belly.**

Proverbs 22:15 — **Foolishness is bound in the heart of a child; but the rod of correction shall drive it far from him.**

Proverbs 23:13,14 — **Withhold not correction from the child: for if thou beatest him with the rod, he shall not**

---

[1] JAMES H. STRONG. *STRONG'S EXHAUSTIVE CONCORDANCE.* COMPACT ED. (GRAND RAPIDS: BAKER, 1992), "HEBREW AND CHALDEE DICTIONARY," P. 114, #7836.

die. Thou shalt beat him with the rod, and shalt deliver his soul from hell.

Proverbs 29:15,17 — **The rod and reproof give wisdom: but a child left to himself bringeth his mother to shame.**

Correct thy son, and he shall give thee rest; yea, he shall give delight unto thy soul.

Using the Rod

The word *rod* is from the Hebrew word *shêbet*, which literally means "stick." Dr. Richard Fugate in his classic book, *What the Bible Says About Child Training,* says, "The word 'rod' is a symbol of God's delegated authority to the human race."[2]

This rod refers to the right of rulership of either governments or parents. When the parent uses the instrument specifically designed by God, that triggers a response in the soul of a child. This natural response makes the minor pain experienced in chastisement take on special meaning. No amount of spanking, hitting with the hand or any form of physical abuse will have the same effect.

Using the rod is best because it is a neutral object, not like the hand, which is attached to a person. Hands are for protecting and comforting. Slapping with the hand is an insult to which children will react negatively. They identify such use of the hand as personal rejection, while use of the rod is seen by them as a result of their own rebellion.

Dr. Fugate says: "These verses indicate the rod to be a thin wooden stick like a switch. Of course, the size of the rod should vary with the size of the child. A willow or peach tree branch may be fine for a rebellious two-year-old, but a small hickory rod or dowell rod would be more fitting for a well-muscled teenage boy."[3]

---

[2] (Tempe, Arizona: Altheia, 1980), p.137-138.

[3] Fugate, p. 141.

The purpose behind using the rod is not to beat our children into submission by sheer brute force. The pain received from the narrow rod is more humbling than it is harmful. We are merely making contact with the sensitive layer of skin closest to the surface where the nerve endings are located. There is no defense against it. The more a child tightens up and braces himself, the more the sting increases. When a paddle or belt is used, it becomes a challenge to the guys to prove their manhood by enduring the maximum force. Using the rod eliminates that problem.

God knew exactly what He was doing when He perfectly planned the universe and our salvation and the use of the rod to break willful rebellion in a child.

State laws vary with regard to punishing a child. Check with your local library to find out what is allowable in your state. You have to walk in wisdom.

You need to predetermine the reason you would spank, the instrument you would use for spanking and who would be spanked, as well as when, where and how the spanking would take place — all in line with the Word of God and in accordance with the laws of the land. The Bible says, **...be ye therefore wise as serpents, and harmless as doves.... Walk in wisdom toward them that are without...** (Matt. 10:16; Col.4:5).

Now let me give you some on-the-job training about using the rod.

There is only one part of our anatomy which God made as a place to be struck with the rod of correction. That place is where all our padding is located. This padding isn't there just so we will be able to sit comfortably.

Listen carefully as I repeat a statement make just a few paragraphs earlier: You should only discipline your child with the rod for being in direct rebellion to what he has specifically and repeatedly been told not to do.

You don't discipline your child for something you didn't explain to him repeatedly and specifically. You should have said plainly, "Don't do this. If you do it, you're going to get a swat for it."

As I said before, you don't spank a child for doing something like spilling milk. That can, however, involve some punishment. (We will discuss this topic later in the chapter.)

Again, the rod is a switch. Now I have heard people refer to this instrument with all kinds of names, like a wooden spoon or a bo-bo paddle.

People have asked, "What's the maximum number of times that I should spank my child on any given day and how many swats should I give him?"

The Bible says whatever is not of faith is sin. (Rom. 14:23.) If you can't, with a comfortable and clear conscience, tell someone else how you just disciplined your child, then you are probably doing something wrong. If you have to spank your child more than a couple of times a day, the chances are your child is being provoked to wrath and is not just being rebellious. (Eph. 6:4.) And if you are striking your child more than two or three times with the rod, chances are you aren't just trying to discipline him but are angry and are out of control.

You should teach your child to fear the rod, not your hand. Your child should *never* fear your hand. Remember, your hand is "attached" to your face via your arm.

I remember one night when I had finished disciplining one of my daughters. After I left her bedroom, she called out, "Daddy, come here!" When I walked back in, she pointed to the rod and said, "Get that out of here." I had left it there on the table. I was the guy who had just used that rod on her, yet she called out to me for help. My daughter wasn't afraid of me. I'm not her enemy; I'm her friend. It was the rod she didn't like.

Now my kids have tried to get rid of the rod. They have burned it in the fireplace, put it in the trash compactor, given it to the dog and thrown it away. But I just keep getting another one.

I think one of the reasons God tells parents to use the rod is that we have to keep it someplace in the house and it usually takes some time for us to go and get it. Then that allows us time to calm down.

Too many times children are being struck everywhere on their anatomy except where all their padding is located. I have seen children with welts on them in places where I'm sure the parent wasn't aiming. Some have even had belt marks around their neck and under the back of their shirt. Parents have done such ungodly and crazy things to punish their kids that they could get locked up for pulling stunts like that — and rightfully so. They should never beat their kids that way!

So what are you to do? Get yourself a rod or a little switch. That's Biblical. There is no substitute for using the rod when it's called for.

How To Spank a Preschooler

Is one of your children still a preschooler? If so, let me explain how to spank him. I have had six.

Let's say your preschooler does something wrong, like biting a chunk out of his brother or sister. You say to him, "We don't do that. Come here."

Now my preschooler didn't come willingly, and yours may not either. You will probably have to go and get your child. Then you get the rod that you use for spanking.

You need to sit down, usually in a low chair, and hold your child between your legs. Cross your legs over him so that he can't get away.

Being right-handed, I put my left hand across my child's back, hook it under his armpit and ease him over on his stomach. (Kids won't be doing this willingly; they may be making lots of noise by this time!) The only target I am shooting for now is my kid's rump, which I am about to strike.

I take that little switch in my hand, raise it up and bring it down on his rump two or three times. *Shoosh! Pow!* Then it's over, and I let him loose.

At this point my child may be crying and squalling, with tears running down his cheeks. I let him cry for about thirty seconds; then I pull him back toward me, rest him on my lap and say, "Do you know what you did wrong?"

My children usually knew exactly what they had done: that which they had specifically and repeatedly been told not to do.

Then I say, "Do you promise not to do it again?"

"Yes, Daddy, I do."

"Okay," I say.

I have them to pray and ask God to forgive them; then I have them to ask me to forgive them. After that, I hug their neck, kiss them, pat them on the rump and send them off to play.

Within three minutes this whole experience is over.

Be Wise About Punishment

One time I brought home two formal dresses for my older daughters. I had spent a lot of money on them, and the price tags were still attached. I took them upstairs and hung them in the girls' closet.

That evening when we were at the table eating lasagna, I noticed everybody was there except for Lauren, our baby girl, who was three years old at the time.

I asked where she was and was told she was still upstairs, so I called out to her, "Lauren, honey, come and eat!"

I heard this faint response, "In a minute!"

A few minutes later, I yelled, "Lauren, the food is getting cold!"

"Okay...in a minute!"

When I had finished eating, Lauren still hadn't come downstairs, so I went looking for her. I called out, "Lauren, where are you?"

"I'm in here," she said.

"Where is 'in here'?"

I walked down the hall looking through all the rooms and finally found her. She was in the last bedroom at the end of the hall and sitting on the closet floor. There was a big grin on her face, and she was holding her plastic safety scissors in her hand.

I must tell you, there is a creative flair about Lauren. She loves scissors, pencils, crayons and Crayola markers. She could be wearing five outfits at one time and have lipstick smeared all around her mouth. She knew grunge before grunge was popular.

Looking down at her, I said, "Honey, what are you doing?"

"I'm working."

Then I glanced over and saw those new formals I had hung there earlier. Lauren had *really* been expressing her creative flair by taking her scissors and working on both dresses. She had cut one-inch strips from the hem all the way to the waist and had cut shreds from the wrist to the armpit on the left sleeves. This job had definitely taken both time and diligence with Lauren cutting such straight lines on those dresses. And I could see all the price tags still dangling off the plastic!

I looked down and said, "Honey, we need to go downstairs and eat supper, but we don't need to tell Mommy anything about this right now. Okay?"

While Lauren was eating her lasagna, Denise knew something was wrong because I kept patting Lauren. She asked me, "What are you doing?"

I'm just eating with my baby," I said. "She didn't get to eat with us so I'm just going to eat with her."

When we had finished, I said to Denise, "Honey, we have to go upstairs and look at something. Lauren has been real busy." Then I said, "Lauren, tell Mommy what you've done."

"I've been working!" she said. Then Denise got this panicked look on her face. She went upstairs and saw what happened. Now she didn't go ballistic, but she wasn't too happy!

It seems that, just the week before, Denise had gone to Wal-Mart to buy some shiny cloth to cut out ribbons for the girls. She had been sitting at the sewing machine cutting strips of that cloth, and Lauren had been watching her every day.

So Lauren wasn't meaning to be malicious or destructive; she was just working the way she had seen her mommy work.

There was a time in my life as a father, even a serious-minded Christian, when, after finding Lauren in that closet, I would have jerked her up by her wrist and worn out her bottom with my hand. And by doing that, I would have been severely and grossly in sin. But thank God for His Word and for the wisdom of His Word. Scripture calls wisdom **the stability of thy times** (Isa. 33:6).

I could have given some harsh punishment to my three-year-old, but instead I spent time repeatedly explaining to Lauren that she didn't ever want to do that again.

And God bountifully provided the money for us to buy two more formals.

Punishing Older Kids

Let's say you have older kids. As an example, let's picture the same situation occurring in two different families and being handled in two different ways.

An Angry Dad

Suppose Dad is looking forward to watching a big college football game Saturday afternoon on TV. With a wife and two boys in the house, he works hard to provide for his family. He had worked about sixty hours that week — and now it's Saturday. It had been a long week and he was tired, so he was still upstairs asleep.

When the older boy wakes up, he goes downstairs and starts looking for something to eat. There isn't much left — just a bowl of Cheerios and a little bit of milk — so he fills a bowl, sits down and starts watching MTV, while eating the cereal.

Then Junior wakes up and goes downstairs, holding a blanket in one hand and a teddy bear in the other. He wants something to eat too, but the cereal box and the milk carton are empty. So he walks over to his big brother and says, "I'm hungry."

But his big brother only replies, "Kid, get out of here!"

"Hey, you got all the cereal!" he complains. "I want something to eat too!"

Unsympathetic, Big Brother merely responds with, "I said for you to get out of here!"

That makes Junior mad, so he lunges at his brother. The bowl of cereal flies into the air and crashes onto the kitchen floor. Then they begin to duke it out. Big Brother wants to punch out Junior's lights, while Junior tries to bite chunks of flesh out of his big brother.

Then Mom wakes up and hears all the noise going on downstairs. She rolls over, pokes on Dad and says, "Get up! Something's going on downstairs!"

Concerned about what might be happening, Dad jumps out of bed, runs around the foot of the bed and heads down the hall.

The boys can hear their dad moving upstairs, and they know that Atilla the Hun has been raised from the dead! So both of them jump up off the floor and take off, with Junior running out the back door and Big Brother heading out the front.

As Dad comes around the corner into the kitchen, his feet hit the milk and cereal that are spread across the linoleum floor. *Wham!* Down he goes! Then that sticky mess is attached to his back.

That gets Dad *really* mad! He jumps up and runs out the front door, a stream of foul words pouring from his mouth. So there he is, standing in the front yard on a Saturday morning in only his underwear, with cereal pressed to his back, and he is cussing a blue streak!

Suddenly, he realizes that some of the neighborhood ladies are outside working in their yards, while some of the dads are out doing chores — and they can see him and hear him! So he turns and runs back into the house.

Meeting his wife in the foyer, he yells out, "You raised two idiots!" Then he runs upstairs, gets dressed, goes down to the beer joint and drinks enough beer that afternoon to get so plastered that he passes out.

Dad's favorite team wins by a point at the very last of the game — and he misses the whole thing!

A Righteous Father

Down the street lives a righteous father who also has been working hard that week. But he hasn't been so busy that he has forsaken the Body of Christ. He still helps by being a blessing to his pastor and his church. By learning the Word of God, he is growing in God's grace and knowledge.

This dad also has two boys. He too is looking forward to the big football game that Saturday, and he too is upstairs asleep.

Big Brother gets up, goes downstairs and mixes the last of the cereal and milk. He turns on the TV in the kitchen to watch the big tractor pull. *Whoommmm! Vrooommm!* He is having a big time.

Then Junior gets up and goes downstairs. He wants some food too, but his big brother got it all and won't share.

Then Big Brother says, "Get out of here!"

That makes Junior mad, so he lunges at Big Brother and knocks the cereal bowl out of his hand. When it hits the floor, milk runs all over the linoleum and Cheerios go everywhere. Then they start swinging at one another.

Christians can duke it out too. Do you ever go to some Christian ball games? Unfortunately, they can fight and cuss one another just like the world does. Some denominations seem more "anointed" than others when it comes to that kind of behavior.

When the fighting starts, Mom wakes up, slaps her husband on the back and says, "Hey, wake up!" He gets out of bed, stretches himself and puts on his pants like a civilized man. He walks around the corner of the bed and stops off at the bathroom for a minute. Then he goes downstairs.

As Dad comes down the stairs, the kids don't even hear him. (As Isaiah 28:16 says, the righteous don't make haste.) Then all of a sudden they see him and say, "Oh, no! Dad's up!"

But do they run from him? No! They just stand there, waiting. They know better than to run from Dad. (Proverbs 28:1 says that the wicked flee when no man pursues and the righteous are as bold as a lion.) A child should be taught to never run from his dad!

Dad goes straight to the pantry where he keeps the rod hanging on the wall. Then he walks back into the room and says simply, "Okay, what's the problem? What happened?"

Pointing at Junior, Big Brother says, "Look what he did — he broke that cereal bowl!"

Then Junior says, "But I'm hungry, Daddy! He got all the cereal and wouldn't give me any of it!"

Dad says, "Okay, that's enough."

Then he looks at the older boy and says, "Bend over," so the boy bends over the kitchen table. The boy knows this isn't going to feel good because, during the fight, his pajamas got soaked with milk.

Still sleepy, Dad yawns. But holding the rod in his hand, he pulls back his arm and comes down hard with it on the boy's backside. *Swoosh!*

Then Daddy turns to the younger brother and says, "Now it's your turn," and he gives the boy one hard strike on his backside. *Swoosh!*

Giving the boys a little time to get some feeling back down to their feet, Dad walks to the pantry to hang up the rod. Then he comes back, looks at the older boy and says, "Okay, son, what do you have to say for yourself?"

"I'm sorry, Dad. I should have done what the Bible says: *Do unto others as you would have others do unto you.*[4] I should have let my little brother have the rest of my cereal."

"That's right, son; you should have. Now Junior, what should you have done?"

"I should have done what the Bible says and let my big brother keep that cereal."

"That's right, son; you should have. Now let's pray together."

When they have knelt down, Dad says to Junior, "Okay, you pray first."

Junior prays, "Father, forgive me for being a jerk and beating up on my big brother. I'm sorry. In Jesus' name. Amen."

Then Dad has his older son to pray a prayer.

When finished, Dad stands up, hugs and kisses both boys and says to them, "Now I want you to clean up this mess before your Mom sees it."

Dad goes back upstairs, walks around the end of the bed, hangs up his pants and gets under the bed covers. Pulling them up around his neck, he looks over at his wife and says, "The ball game comes on at noon. Would you wake me up at 11:30? I don't want to miss any of the game." Then he falls off to sleep.

---

[4] SEE MATTHEW 7:12; LUKE 6:31.

There is the righteous way, and then there is a way that will make the parent look like the north end of a southbound mule. And all of the neighbors will know which kind he is.

The Past Is Past

Micah 6:8 — **...and what doth the Lord require of thee, but to do justly, and to love mercy....**

To do justly requires that you know God's Word and apply it in your daily living.

To love mercy means for you to be forgiving. If your child repents about something, you need to forgive and get on with life.

Unfortunately, mothers have memories like elephants. They can remember everything, and they always want to bring up the past. They can remind their child of something he had done years before, saying, "I remember when you did that three years ago. I remember what you were wearing and who you were with at the time."

Once you have repented of your sins, the Bible says your sins have been removed from you as far as the east is from the west and will be cast into the depths of the sea. (Ps. 103:12; Mic. 7:19.) God doesn't remember past sins and He won't keep bringing them up to you.

So if your child did something in the past, don't keep bringing it up. The past is past. Get on with life in the future.

Three Rules in Our Home

We have three rules in our home to point out to our kids things they absolutely cannot do. These rules can be found displayed throughout our house: on a big piece of poster board, on the bedroom wall, on the refrigerator, on the bathroom mirror.

Rule #1: Don't ever talk back to Mom and Dad.

This is an absolute no-no!

As I say to my kids: "If you can talk back to me, you'll talk back to your teacher. By talking back to your teacher, you'll be in trouble all the time. Then if you start talking back to your boss, it will get you fired, and I'll have to support you for the rest of your life."

Rule #2: Don't argue with your brother and sisters.

I tell my children: "If you can't get along with your brother and sisters, you won't be able to get along with your fellow students and you'll just be staying in trouble. You'll never be able to keep a job because you'll always be fighting with your fellow workers, and I'll be supporting you all your life."

Rule #3: Nobody tells a lie.

Jesus said, "I am the truth," (John 14:6.) The Word says that the devil is a liar and the father of all liars and that liars will be found in hell. (John 8:44; Rev. 21:8.)

I tell my children: "Even the worst sinner you have ever met hates a liar. Nobody — whether sinner or saint — likes a liar. But it seems the easiest thing for a human to do is to tell a lie. So always tell the truth."

Rules and Rewards

In discipline, parents need to do two things for their children:

1. Set rules for them to follow.

2. Have some rewards for their obedience to those rules.

At our house I have to make sure I am enforcing whatever rules I have made. Sometimes voices get raised. With as many people as there are in our house, words can fly at a rapid pace sometimes. But I know when they have reached a certain place

and are about to pass the point of no return. T
my hands and say, "Time out!" I give the last wo.

Rewards are important. Children need some k
even if it's just a little sticker on a chart. Then their
little smoother. So find something as a reward, like i\ __\am, for
instance. Just be sure it's something you can afford.

Ask God and believe Him to reward your children. As
Scripture says, God is the rewarder. Hebrews 11:6 says, ...**he is a
rewarder of them that diligently seek him.** In the book of
Revelation, He says, **To him that overcometh will I give...** (Rev.
2:7,17).

You need to have certain rules that you are gong to enforce consistently. But don't have too many rules for your children to follow.

Never Call Your Kid an Idiot

Don't be yelling at your child and calling him stupid. He will
start thinking, *I must be an idiot because my dad said I am.*

While sitting in school one day, suppose he hears the teacher
call one of the other kids stupid. Looking at that kid, he thinks,
There's one just like me. So he goes over and sits down next to him,
thinking: *He's stupid and I'm stupid, so we can be stupid together.
We'll go to stupid places, do stupid things, listen to stupid music and talk
like stupid people, because we both are stupid.*

As Scripture says:

Proverbs 18:21 — **Death and life are in the power of the
tongue: and they that love it shall eat the fruit thereof.**

Speak Good Words Over Your Kids

It's important that you speak good words over your children.
Say, "I call those things that be not as though they were." (Rom.
4:17.) Speak words over your kids like those spoken to Gideon

David: "You are a mighty man (or woman) of valor, and you will do great things for God." (See Judg. 6:12, 1 Sam. 26:25.)

Even if your child just bombed out on a test or got caught talking the third time in study hall, you have to continue seeing him or her as God's champion.

There are times when you will have to discipline your child, but always follow it by saying, "Everything's going to be fine. The sun will still come up. God's mercies are new every morning. Life will go on."

If you will do that consistently, you won't have to spank your kids as much, and they will love your for it. God's peace will be in your home.

But if you don't do what the Word says, you will be heading toward child abuse. God doesn't want you to abuse your kids. He loves your kids and He needs them.

As we read in Micah 6:8, you are to do justly, but the only way you can do justly is by putting God's Word inside you. You need to be involved in church, listening to your pastor and fellowshipping together with other believers. You won't be going through things that someone else has not already gone through. There is nothing new under the sun. So realize God has answers for you.

But remember the statement I made at the beginning of this chapter: You will never successfully discipline your kids if you don't have a relationship with them. Now that can take some time, so just be patient. Don't try to change everything in one night.

Suggestion for Reading

I want to recommend to you Dr. Richard Fugate's book on the subject of training your kids, which I have quoted in this chapter. It's entitled *What the Bible Says About Child Training*. This is a very good book. It's based on the Word of God and is easy reading, using big print and lots of pictures.

Many times when counseling parents who are having discipline problems, I have given them a copy of this book. I tell them to go home, read it and then call me. After reading this book ninety percent of those parents have called and said they didn't need to come back in for more counseling because they had found their answer.

A Prayer for Repentance

Now maybe you have done wrong in raising your kids. I want to give you an opportunity to repent right now. Every parent has done wrong to some extent; we all make mistakes. Many of us have ignorantly tried to parent our kids the way we have seen the world do it.

If you have done that, I just want you to give it to God and ask Him to forgive you of any wrong, of any sin, of any abuse you may have committed against your kids. You need to get that feeling of guilt off your back right now. Get the devil out of your life and don't give him any place anymore.

Insert your name in the prayer below, and read it believing that God will move mightily on your behalf:

Father, there are many parents who have done wrong and feel guilty for it, with the devil trying to condemn them. But, Father, right now _____, the person reading this prayer, is coming before You in the name of Jesus to confess his or her sins. He/She is admitting now that he/she has done wrong concerning his/her children, but he/she is repenting of it and turning from it. _____ has heard the truth; and not only has the truth set him/her free, but it will keep him/her free.

_____ will not abuse his/her children but will love them and train them properly according to Your Word. He/She is going to do righteously. Therefore, his/her children will grow up strong and healthy in their bodies and be filled with Your wisdom and Your knowledge in their minds. They will be mighty in their spirits and strengthened by the power of the Holy Ghost in their inner man.

Father, I thank You now for the forgiving power and the cleansing blood of Jesus that is coming over _____'s life as he/she has repented before You.

Now that You have forgiven him/her, Father, I ask that You give him/her bucketfuls of practical wisdom for successful daily living concerning his/her children.

I remind You of Your Word which says this is Your child; therefore, the love of God has been shed abroad in his/her heart by the Holy Ghost. He/She has Your love and Your grace. He/She has the patience, the wisdom and the power within him/her to live and do righteously concerning his/her children.

Father, with whatever is going on in his/her life, Your grace is more than sufficient. Some receive more than others, but some need more than others. Father I thank You that many lives are being changed and people are making a 180-degree turn to go in the other direction in their relationship with their children. I thank You now for continuing that work.

I believe that which You have begun, Father, You will continue to do. I look forward to the future of our children, in Jesus' name. Praise God!

7

Favor With God = Stewardship

Luke 2:52 — And Jesus increased in wisdom and stature, and in *favour with God* and man.

The third part of this verse I want us to look at is:

And Jesus increased in...*favour with God....*

This means God was pleased with Him. The word I want to use for *favor with God* is *stewardship.*

Jesus growing in favor with God means He was a wise steward over everything He had — His gifts, His talents, His abilities.

A Parable About Stewardship

How do you have favor with God? In Matthew 25, Jesus talks about the parable of the talents.

Matthew 25:14-20 — For the kingdom of heaven is as a man travelling into a far country, who called his own servants, and delivered unto them his goods.

And unto one he gave five talents, to another two, and to another one; to every man according to his several ability; and straightway took his journey.

Then he that had received the five talents went and traded with the same, and made them other five talents.

And likewise he that had received two, he also gained other two.

But he that had received one went and digged in the earth, and hid his lord's money.

After a long time the lord of those servants cometh, and reckoneth with them.

And so he that had received five talents came and brought other five talents, saying, Lord, thou deliveredst unto me five talents: behold, I have gained beside them five talents more.

Notice that in verse 15 it says the talents were given **to every man according to his several ability.** This obviously means that each of them had different abilities.

In this parable Jesus tells about a servant who took five talents and made five more. When the servant reports this to his lord, he is praised. The story continues:

Matthew 25:21 — **His lord said unto him, Well done, thou good and faithful servant: thou hast been faithful over a few things, I will make thee ruler over many things: enter thou into the joy of thy Lord.**

These same words were spoken to the servant who had two talents and made two more. (See vv. 22,23.)

But the servant who had one talent didn't use it. He went and buried it. (See vv. 24,25.) If you don't use it, you lose it.

Matthew 25:26-29 — **His lord answered and said unto him, Thou wicked and slothful servant, thou knewest that I reap where I sowed not, and gather where I have not strawed:**

Thou oughtest therefore to have put my money to the exchangers, and then at my coming I should have received mine own with usury.

Take therefore the talent from him, and give it unto him which hath ten talents.

For unto every one that hath shall be given, and he shall have abundance: but from him that hath not shall be taken away even that which he hath.

What we have here is an illustration of stewardship. We read how two out of three people in this parable had favor with God. I want to please God by being a wise steward over what He has given me.

God is big on stewardship, so you need to be teaching your children how to handle their gifts, talents and money.

You may say, "But we don't have any money."

That means your kids never will have any if they don't learn how to handle it. Until you are able to steward it, you will never get any. (This subject will be covered in greater detail in a later chapter.)

Teach Your Children About Giving

Every Sunday as we were going into Sunday school, I would stick my hand into my pocket and take out some nickels and dimes for my children to give as their offering.

As I was handing them the change, I would say, "Here's *your* offering, and *your* offering, and *your* offering." I was so proud to be sending them into church with an offering to give.

One morning after doing this, I went into church and sat down in the pew. As the service was about to start, God began speaking to my spirit. He said, "Son, do you know what you're doing?"

"Yes, Lord, I'm getting ready to have church. I feel really good about it. It's the first Sunday this month that we made it on time."

He said, "But you're teaching your children to give Me pocket change."

"What?"

He said it again: "You are teaching your children to give Me pocket change. When your children are grown and the plate is passed in church, they will drop in a few dollars and feel so good about it. But, son, if you don't ever get your kids on My financial plan of giving, they may work hard but never really have anything."

There is only one way to have anything on this planet: by sowing and reaping.

As the Bible says, **...with what measure ye mete, it shall be measured to you...** (Mark 4:24).

Let me give you my own translation of this Scripture verse: "The measuring stick you use to give will be the same measuring stick God uses to give back to you."

If you give a teaspoonful, when God gets ready to give back to you, He will pick up His heavenly teaspoon to use in giving back to you. But it will be good measure, pressed down, shaken together and running over in that teaspoon.

If you give a tablespoonful, He will pick up His heavenly tablespoon, fill it up and give back to you good measure, pressed down, shaken together and running over.

If you pick up an ice-bucket shovel to use in your giving, He will give an ice-bucket shovelful back to you.

And if you give only pocket change, you will receive pocket change in return.

That's a Bible principle. The measure you use to give is the same measure God uses to give back to you.

So if you don't give your children money now, they will never learn how to save it and manage it. You have to be a good steward over it.

Being Faithful Over Little

As Jesus said in this parable, he that is faithful over little shall be made ruler over much. (Matt. 25:21.) That means the person who isn't faithful over even a little will always wish he had much; but he will have nothing because he doesn't know how to be faithful over that little bit.

Are you griping because you don't have a new car? Why don't you go home and wash the old one that you have now?

Do you want a bigger house? Why don't you go home and fix up the one you live in now?

Being faithful over little will make you ruler over much.

Our society wants everything now. People say, "I want nice...big...new — now!"

That's why the average American family each year spends four hundred dollars more than it earns. Personal consumer debt increases at the rate of one thousand dollars per second. This debt has now reached such a level that 23 percent of take-home pay for the average American is already committed to paying existing debt, not including the home mortgage. Eighty percent of American people owe more than they own; only 2 percent are financially self-sustaining. And most sobering, a recent poll found that 56 percent of all divorces were related to financial tensions in the home.[1]

People are up to their eyeballs in debt and can't get out. Now if you think things are tough on us today, what do you think life will be like for our children if Jesus tarries?

But my Bible says:

Psalm 112:1-3 — **Praise ye the Lord. Blessed is the man that feareth the Lord, that delighteth greatly in his commandments.**

His seed shall be mighty upon earth: the generation of the upright shall be blessed.

Wealth and riches **shall be in his house: and his righteousness endureth for ever.**

---

[1] *Husbands and Wives* (Wheaton, Illinois: Victor, 1988), pp. 399,412.

Don't look to see if your sister, brother or neighbor believes this; they may not. So why don't you believe it and set the pace?

It's like running in a race. When you can see a lot of people running alongside you, you know you aren't doing too good. But when you look around and can't see anybody, that means you are out in front and doing good.

So don't look around to see if anyone is doing what you are doing. There won't be very many. You be the pacesetter; get out in front and just keep running.

Giving Must Be a Habit

Now I don't want to downplay any one of the four topics we are discussing in this book. All four subjects tie together. You can have a vision for your life and you can be really self-disciplined; but if you are always broke, life is just a bummer.

You have to learn to be a giver. It's a habit to be developed. There are some people who go through life trying to hold on to it, but they never have anything. Then there are those who go through life giving it away, and they just don't know what to do with all of it; it just keeps coming back on them.

In the next few chapters we will look at four areas having to do with your child:

1. Self-esteem.

There are seminars on this subject being held all over the country. This is a legitimate term, and we will be looking at it briefly from the Bible.

2. Your child's gift from God.

At the moment of conception every child is gifted by God to do and succeed at something in this life.

3. Your child's money.

Money is something we all need, by the way. If you don't have any, life can be tough. But if you don't know how to handle even a little of it, you will never have much more. The way more money comes to you is by being faithful over what little you have now.

4. Teaching your child about work.

Every child should learn how to work. As Scripture says, if we don't work, we don't eat. (2 Thess. 3:10.) Eating is definitely a good thing to do, and we won't live long without it. So you have to know how to work and then teach your children about it.

Work is part of what God talked about to Adam in the book of Genesis. He said, "Adam, you're going to have to work by the sweat of your brow if you want to produce anything." (Gen. 3:19.) Another Scripture says, **The hand of the diligent shall bear rule...** (Prov. 12:24).

Let's look now at the subject of self-esteem. This is valuable for *every* believer. Parents have to learn it first and then teach it to their kids.

8

The Importance of Self-Esteem

We need to get a mental picture of the fact that God has placed us on this planet at this time for a specific purpose. It isn't just by accident or happenstance that we were born in this generation and are living and breathing in this very day and hour. We are here by divine appointment. God knows we are here and He wants to use us. He has gifts and talents for each and every member of the Body of Christ.

In Luke 6:46 Jesus asks the question, "Why do you call Me Lord and don't do what I say?"

Low self-esteem is nothing more than failing to do what we know is right. The Bible calls it righteousness! Romans 14:17 reads: **For the kingdom of God is not meat and drink; but righteousness** (doing what is right), **and peace, and joy in the Holy Ghost.** We can't do what is right until we know what is right. Once we know the truth (what is right), the truth will make us free. (John 8:32.) As Jesus said, without Him we can do nothing. (John 15:5.)

That's why God gave us the Law in the Old Testament. It was to make obvious to all of us that we, in ourselves, are out of right relationship with God and to show us the futility of creating some religious system of getting by our own efforts what we can only get by faith in God and His promises.

You know, there is no single factor that has more influence on how successful our children are in school or in the schooling process than what they think about themselves. Proverbs 23:7

says, as someone thinks in his heart, so is he. We act the way we think, and we think about what we feed on. Self-esteem starts with knowing and then doing the Word of God.

Now let me ask you a question: What if Jesus tarries another few years before coming again as He promised that He would and doesn't come back in our generation? We must make sure that the things God has asked us to do are passed on to the next generation.

In Israel today, every teenager — both male and female — serves in the military. Why? Because their country is surrounded by its enemies. This is urgent to the Israelis. They don't sit around and debate the issue; it isn't debatable. Their enemies are plotting to kill them night and day, so life is serious for them, and they are surviving.

The Israelis have a different mentality. It's almost like they are concerned with their next generation. We can read in the Old Testament how God was concerned about future generations; He told parents to get involved with their kids.

Get Involved With *Your* Next Generation

As parents today, we need to be concerned with the next generation. We need to work at training our kids, praying for them and passing on to them what we know about God's principles, that they may increase and not diminish. God spoke this to Israel years ago, and He is saying it to His Church today.

In his classic book, *Educational Ideals in the Ancient World*, William Barclay wrote these words[1]:

> In history no nation has ever set the child in the midst more deliberately than the Jews did. It would not be wrong to say that for the Jew the child was the most important person in the community. The Jew was sure that, of all people, the child was dearest to God. In First

---

[1] (GRAND RAPIDS: BAKER, 1959), PP. 11,13,15,16.

Chronicles 16:22, where we read, "Touch not mine anointed, and do my prophets no harm," "touch not mine anointed" referred to school children; and "do my prophets no harm" to their teachers. The Talmud says, "So long as there are children in the schools, Israel's enemies cannot prevail against her." It has to be remembered that Jewish education was entirely religious education. There was no textbook except the Scriptures, and the aim was to train up its disciples in the way of God. The responsibility for educating children was laid fairly and squarely on the parents, and that was true in the days when there were schools, just as much as in the days before schools came into being.

A person cannot inherit their parents' knowledge the same as they might their fortune. The knowledge is there, but each generation has to win it and enter into it for itself. That's why as a parent we must always be able and ready and willing to tell our children the great things that God has done for us.

The education or knowledge to be passed on to the Jewish child was both religious and vocational. Concerning the religious education, on the very first day of school young Jewish boys were wakened before dawn, bathed and dressed in a gown with fringes. The boy's father then took him to the synagogue, and he was put on the reading desk with the roll opened in front of him at Exodus 20:2-26, the passage that tells of God's revelation of the Law to Moses. The passage was read aloud as the passage for the day. He was then taken to the house of his teacher, who showed him a slate with the alphabet written on it in various combinations with two of the basic texts of the Law. In addition to that, there was one further sentence: "The Law will be my calling." These things the teacher read to the boy, and the boy repeated them after the teacher. The slate was then smeared with honey, and the boy was told to lick it off. This was in memory of

Ezekiel's experience when he ate the roll: "And it was in my mouth as honey for sweetness." (Ezek. 3:1-3.) Then the boy was given sweet cakes to eat, with passages from the Law in praise of the Law written on them. You can see how this would leave a lifetime impression on the boy. It was as if to say this Law, this Word of God, will become your very life, your very existence.

Concerning the vocational education, the father had a duty to teach his son a trade, for the Talmud says: "Whosoever does not teach his son a trade teaches him to steal." The threefold duty of the father was to instruct his son in the Law, to bring him into wedlock and to teach him a handicraft. (Prov. 1:8; 4:1-4; 6:20; 13:1.)

If we really believe this, we would be consumed with seeing this message passed on. We would be training up our children to carry on the message of Jesus Christ. It makes no difference what their vocation may be, whether preachers, electricians, plumbers, doctors, lawyers or some other profession. Our children still must carry the message of Jesus Christ into the next generation while earning a living for themselves and their families.

You Can Receive From God Now

Most of God's people today are just trying to hang on and survive. The world has pumped so much unbelief into us. We are just working at surviving this day, this week, this month, this pay period. But that's not the will of God. We have been listening to a lie.

That's why Romans 12:2 tells us that every day we have to start renewing our mind. We have to think like God thinks. How does He think? *Very* big!

You might be saying, "Well, maybe I need to ask God for something." According to James 4:2, **...ye have not, because ye ask not.** As Jesus said in John 16:24, **...ask, and ye shall receive, that your joy may be full.**

So then you say, "Okay, I'm going to ask."

But there is a bonus in heaven. God is saying, "If you ask, I will do above and beyond all you could ask or think." Ephesians 3:20 says, **Now unto him that is able to do exceeding abundantly above all that we ask or think....**

God is looking to and fro throughout the earth to find people to whom He can show Himself strong. (2 Chron. 16:9.)

Are you a candidate for receiving from God? When you are weak, say, "I am strong." Say: "Lord, here I am. As Jesus said, without Him I can do absolutely, positively, 100 percent nothing. But I have Him today; therefore, all things are possible to me as one who believes." (John 15:5; Mark 9:23.)

This is an attitude. Some people have stolen these principles and converted them into "positive-thinking seminars." They are making millions of dollars by going around the country preaching on positive thinking, telling people how life would be better if they just changed their attitudes.

This is true. But why don't you put God's Word in your heart and keep it before your eyes? (Prov. 4:20-22.) The Word of God is better than a positive attitude. God watches over His Word to perform it. (Jer. 1:12 AMP.)

Your positive attitude is a part of it, but you need to watch and see which road you are going down. All roads may lead to the same destination, but their paths can vary. Some will get you there quicker than others, while some will take you off to wander through the swamp.

I want my children to know about stewardship so they will be able to take care of what they have.

Teaching Stewardship to Your Children

Let me share some statistics that will show the importance of teaching stewardship to your kids.

127

Several years ago Moody Bible Institute did a study on the ages that people became born-again believers, confessing Jesus Christ as their Lord and Savior. They determined that 86 percent came to know the Lord before age fifteen; 10 percent between ages fifteen and thirty; but only four percent after the age of thirty.[2]

In every evangelistic program I have ever been involved with, we were knocking on doors and trying to reach those people over thirty. We worked hard for that 4 percent. Never have so many worked so much for so few. We didn't bother with children; we didn't think they could really understand anyway.

The denomination I grew up in didn't allow kids to take communion until age twelve. They didn't think children really understood it. So by the time I was twelve, I had just about made up my mind about God. The only reason we wanted to "get saved" anyhow was so we could take communion; then we would be able to get all those shot glasses and act like we were getting drunk.

As Isaiah 28:9 tells us, we have to start teaching our children the doctrines of God when they are weaned from their mothers. If we wait until they turn twelve before trying to teach them God's Word, the world will have all that time to work on them; and much of a child's character is set by age twelve.

It's not what kids know but how they react to pressure. You show me how a child reacts at age seven, and I will show you how he will react at ages seventeen and forty-seven. People will always react the same. It's a habit, a learned skill. For them to be any different requires a heart change.

Now stewardship is critical here if these statistics are true.

When Jesus taught His disciples about the fields being white unto harvest, He was saying, "Don't look ahead for the harvest; the harvest is here and now." (Author's paraphrase; see John 4:35.)

---

[2] GRACE FELLOWSHIP EDUCATION DEPARTMENT TEACHER'S MANUAL (TULSA, OKLAHOMA: GRACE FELLOWSHIP CHURCH, 1988), P. 2.

Of the 5.6 billion people on this planet, it's estimated that 30 percent of them are under the age of eighteen.[3] That means over one-and-one-half billion people today are kids. The field is ready to be harvested!

Kids Are Born To Believe

Now my kids are born to believe. When my son was three, if I had told him there was a pink elephant in the backyard, he would have believed me. He would have run to the window, put his nose against the pane and asked, "Where's the pink elephant, Dad?" Then I would have said, "Just kidding, son." The truth is, I would have been lying.

Children learn about lying and about deceit. They are born to believe, so they are going to believe something.

As an example, when the communists took over in Cuba, one important thing they did was to take over the school systems. They took all the kids out of schools and began teaching them about communism. Those kids were indoctrinated. Every non-Christian knows a child learns a little bit at a time, so they worked on those kids a little bit at a time. That's how they learned.

The most important thing with stewardship is to pass on principles to others. There are several principles involved, like faith, for instance. Our faith is the most important thing we can pass on to our children.

Self-Esteem Is a Must

Self-esteem has become a big buzz word, but it's a legitimate word. Let's look at a great passage of Scripture from Ephesians 5.

---

[3] THESE FIGURES ARE BASED ON THE POPULATION OF THE SIX LARGEST COUNTRIES: CHINA, RUSSIA, INDIA, MEXICO, BRAZIL AND THE USA, AS TAKEN FROM THE 1995 WORLD ALMANAC.

There is something hidden here that you might be surprised to see. The Scripture says:

> Ephesians 5:24-29 — **Therefore as the church is subject unto Christ, so let the wives be to their own husbands in every thing.**
>
> **Husbands, love your wives, even as Christ also loved the church, and gave himself for it;**
>
> **That he might sanctify and cleanse it with the washing of water by the word,**
>
> **That he might present it to himself a glorious church, not having spot, or wrinkle, or any such thing; but that it should be holy and without blemish.**
>
> **So ought men to love their wives as their own bodies. He that loveth his wife loveth himself.**
>
> **For no man ever yet hated his own flesh; but nourisheth and cherisheth it, even as the Lord the church.**

Again, verse 28 says: **So ought men to love their wives as their own bodies. He that loveth his wife loveth himself.**

Many times when couples have come to me for counseling, the wife sits there and says, "I wish somebody would teach my husband how to love me more." Whenever I hear that, I just mark it down: *Wife is here about husband/Husband has bad case of low self-esteem.*

A husband can't love his wife anymore than he loves himself. If he feels crummy about himself, that's how he will treat his wife. He can't treat her any better than he thinks about himself. Now this isn't conceit; it's just a fact of human life.

The most successful people you will ever meet in this world are people who really know themselves — their good points and their bad points — and they like who they are. They are good folks; they feel comfortable about who they are and good about what they do. They aren't trying to be something they are not.

Today we can hear it said that wealthy people have either "old money" or "new money." People who have had money for a long time can usually dress casually because they aren't trying to impress other people. On the other hand, those with "new money" always dress up in fancy clothes, trying to show others that they have money, too. Then there are those who try to make people think they have money when they really don't. They just keep themselves in debt in order to be like the Jones.

You can't love your children any more than you love yourself. You have to find out how God sees you and start seeing yourself the same way.

God sees us, not for what we are, but for what we are going to become, because He sees us through the eyes of His Son Jesus Christ, Who paid a high price for us. He sees us redeemed, righteous, justified and sanctified. If He sees us that way, then why should we see ourselves any differently?

Our Enemy, the Devil

You need to remember though that we have an enemy, who is always working against God's people. He goes by the names, *Satan* and *the devil*.

Our enemy is the liar of all liars. In John 8:44, Jesus described the devil as the father of lies. In Revelation 12:10, he is called the accuser of the brethren.

It's the devil's job to come at you and me, at my child and your child, and always be telling us how worthless, no-good, stupid, ugly and dumb we are. That's his job, and he's good at it!

Free From Condemnation

But as Scripture says, **There is therefore now no condemnation to them which are in Christ Jesus...** (Rom. 8:1). We don't have to feel condemned by the devil.

I know what I once was, but I also know what I am now. **Therefore if any man be in Christ, he is a new creature: old things are passed away; behold, all things are become new** (2 Cor. 5:17). Now this doesn't mean I was made perfect. Even though I am righteous through Christ Jesus, I can stumble and fall on my face seven times a day. But it's my job to get back up, dust myself off, repent and keep moving on.

When I ask God to forgive me, He will. He removes that sin from me as far as the east is from the west and casts it into the depths of the sea. He sees me free from sin! (Ps. 103:12; Mic. 7:19.)

If I start bringing up things I have done, He will say, "But I don't remember that."

"Sure You do, Lord. I just did that yesterday. Remember?"

"No, you have repented of it," He says, "and I can't remember it."

God cannot lie. (Tit. 1:2.) If He says He doesn't remember it, He isn't lying to you or kidding with you. So don't be reminding Him of it.

He says, "I don't remember your sin; you repented of that, so don't keep bringing it up."

"But I remember it, Lord, and I feel crummy about it."

That would be like saying all that Jesus did wasn't worth anything. If you have repented, then it's done — period. It was buried under His blood. Don't be sticking your hand down into the pot, grabbing that sin and dragging it back out.

You have to see yourself this way before you can really see your kids in a certain way.

Three Ways to Self-Esteem

Now I am going to give you three ways that can be used to enhance either yourself, your spouse or your child. But I will be dealing mainly with your child's self-esteem. How do you get your kid to feel good about himself? Here are the three ways:

1. Communicate and Listen — Be Slow To Speak and Quick To Hear (James 1:19).

Parents are all the time saying to me, "I've tried to talk to my kids about that, but they won't even listen."

Let me tell you, Mom and Dad, you will never be able to have a deep conversation with your child if you don't first have some idiot conversations with him. If you aren't willing to listen to all the dumb things your kids have to say, you will never be able to talk to them about the important things. It's called communicating.

I have learned to be a good listener. Sometimes when my children start talking to me, everything sounds so silly. I feel like saying to them: "I'm too busy to listen right now. I have some important things to think about, so you just sit down and be still." But that's no good. I have to be willing to listen to them.

Let me give you a Scripture:

Proverbs 20:5 — **Counsel in the heart of man is like deep water; but a man of understanding will draw it out.**

I have to look at all six of my kids and know that God has put a gift inside each of them. I don't necessarily know the gifts they have, because I don't have revelation on it. God has to show me like He shows them.

I know, however, that, as I listen to my children, out of the abundance of the heart the mouth will speak. (Matt. 12:34.) The desires of each child will be expressed. By listening to them, I will find out what they are interested in. Then I will know what to start praising about them. I want to start promoting my children and what they do, so I make comments like, "You know, you're really good at that, honey."

I read a story about an artist in which he tells how God gave him the ability and the talent but that his mom put wings to the gift. When his mom came home one day, she found that her little boy had taken out the ink bottle and had been drawing what he thought were the most beautiful pictures. Of course, he was just scribbling — and he had spilled ink all over everything! Looking back on it, he wondered why his mom didn't give him a good spanking.

But she didn't panic. She walked over and picked up the papers he had been drawing on. Then she said, "Son, I didn't know you could draw so good. That's great!" She must have spent ten minutes just bragging on him. Then she said, "Let's put your pictures up here on the refrigerator to dry, and we'll clean up this mess before your dad gets home."

After that, every time he would draw, his mom just bragged on him. As a result, he became a very famous artist.

Another story was told to me by a businessman who had been away on a trip. He said he had really missed his family. But as soon as he walked in the house, he noticed that trash was running over in the kitchen, and it was the job of his fifteen-year-old son to empty the trash. That son came running up to hug his dad's neck, but before the boy could even touch him, Dad unleashed on him, saying, "How come you haven't emptied the trash? I've been gone for five days! Don't you know that it's your job to empty the trash?"

The son apologized three times on the way up the stairs, saying, "I'm real sorry, Dad." But his dad just increased his ranting and raving.

When they sat down for supper, Dad's stomach started churning as God began dealing with him, saying: "Your son ran up to hug your neck because he has a relationship with you, and you just killed it over some trash that could have been emptied in about thirty seconds." That businessman realized then that he had to change his ways.

If parents don't watch out, they can do little things everyday that can kill their relationship with their child and wound their child's spirit. Parents can still teach and train their children without killing their spirits, but it requires them to be wise stewards.

It's like an ant hill. There are some big red ants here in Oklahoma. You can kick down the ant hill or stick firecrackers in it and blow it up, but by the next day those ants will build it back up again. However, they will only work at rebuilding that hill for so long; then they give up. I have seen it happen. It looks as if they have packed their suitcases and are moving out, as if to say: "There's no reason to rebuild this hill; somebody just keeps kicking it down. Why should we try again? Why make the effort? It's hopeless."

2. Be Willing To Get Involved With Your Child.

I can't emphasize this enough. Proverbs 27:17 says:

Iron sharpeneth iron; so a man sharpeneth the countenance of his friend.

This verse is one of the Scriptures included in our study on friendship later in this book, but the principle can apply here as well.

If I am not involved with my children, I have no idea what is going on in their lives. My conversation with them would then become very shallow, with me asking some question like, "How did school go?" I will have no idea if I don't even know what subjects they are taking.

I wonder how many parents do that. The conversation might go something like this:

"How did it go today?" the parent asks.

"Pretty good," the child responds.

The conversation quickly ends with the parent saying simply, "That's good."

Parents like this don't have any idea what their kids are doing, what subjects they are taking, which teachers they have or who their friends are.

Every year being involved in the basketball games at our Christian school, I have noticed that eighty percent of the parents

135

don't show up for any of those games. To them, basketball time means "dump and run." It's a time when they can *dump* their kids and then *run* in some other direction. They go out to eat, or go to the mall and shop, or go home and spend some time alone. It's like the TV commercial that says, "You pay now — you pay later." Parents who act like this will pay for it eventually.

I believe we have had as close a relationship with some of our high-school kids as they have with their own parents because Denise and I are at so many of their ball games. If I am in town, I will be there. The kids can depend on me.

Our school was involved in cross-country meets, and my children were on the team. Sometimes these competitions were held in Oklahoma City. It's a two-hour drive just to get there, but the race itself takes only thirty-to-forty minutes from start to finish. Besides paying money for fees and tolls, it cost me about twenty seven dollars for McDonald's burgers and fries.

I went to these meets several years in a row and seldom saw another parent from our school. It was the same with basketball games played away from home. The parents would make comments like, "I don't have time to drive all the way over there and back; that would take four hours." Yet those same people have enough time to repeatedly come to my office for counseling and to call me at night, crying over their problems. They just don't have enough time for their kids.

Whenever parents don't have time for their kids, it will eventually cost them.

I can talk to my kids about serious things because they know I love them. As Jesus said, "I know you love Me because you do what I say." (John 14:23.) My kids know when I am at their ball games or other activities. I know when they are strong and when they are weak. I go to encourage them, and they know it.

Even if I am out of town, I can call home and ask my daughter, "How did the game go tonight?"

If she says it didn't go so good, I don't respond by saying, "Well, honey, just try harder. You just hang in there now." Instead, I say, "Tell me what happened."

Once I get some details, and because I know her, I can say: "Do you know what your problem is, honey? You can't dribble without looking down at the ball; you have to keep your head up. We're going to get you some training; then you'll know how to do differently. And after your jump shot, you're too slow coming down the court; you need to pick up some speed." I know what to say because I know my kids.

Denise has said to me many times, "You know, the most important thing we have done as parents is to have been there for our children."

Despite numerous mistakes, the best thing we have ever done was to just plainly be there for them; if not physically, they knew we were there mentally.

When I talk to my kids, I am a normal parent; but because we have a relationship, I can get specific. As the Scripture says, I am like iron sharpening iron. By being specific I am helping them, and they know that. I am not just flapping my gums and blowing air. I know my children. I try to know where their weaknesses are, and I try to point out their strengths too.

I have said to my kids: "Do you know what your problem is, sunshine? You're the most disorganized person God ever made. You just don't know what's coming up tomorrow, and you get hit from the backside too many times. So we're going to get you organized. Now it's no big deal. You'll recover from it, and life will go on."

Then I have taken them to the store and bought some of those little organizing books to help bring some order into their lives.

I know where my children are weak and I know how to sharpen them, so they are getting better. But if I never spent time with them, I wouldn't really know them. The same is true with my wife. If I didn't spend time with her, I wouldn't know her either.

Even after twenty-five years of marriage, I still spend time getting to know her.

Relationship is the key. You really can't practice stewardship until you have established relationship.

3. Help Your Kids To Reflect on Things.

This is how to make your child feel better about himself. It says in Proverbs, "As in water, face reflects face, so the heart of man reflects man." (See Prov. 27:19.)

Take some time to sit down and talk with your children. It might only be for five or ten minutes, but it can be well worth it. Even when I am out of town, I will call long distance and try to talk a few minutes with each of the children.

When I first started traveling, the phone bills were eating me alive, so I got an 800 number that costs only a few dollars a month. I can call from anywhere in the United States for only a few cents a minute. The phone with that 800 number is in the kitchen; so when I call home, one of the children usually answers, and we talk for a while.

Sometimes I have to remind my children about things God does for us. That's what God did with Israel. After doing something big, He would say, "Pile up some rocks right here; I want you to remember what I did for you." Then He had them to look back at the things He had done for them during certain momentous times.

Sometimes you have to think on the goodness of God. Have a conversation with yourself that goes something like this: *Things aren't looking so good now, but God showed up before, remember? That's right. He did, didn't He?* By doing this, you are encouraging yourself in the Lord.

Sometimes when things get tough and one of my kids is going through a trial, I have to make him or her sit down and think for a minute. I say: "Look, we've been through things before, and other people have been through them too. Now let's sit down and think about this. It's just not that big of a deal, so don't let it get you down. God has brought you out before, and He can do it again."

I don't want my children to lose their joy for life, so I turn into a big cheerleader. You know, the only one God ever kicked when he was down was the devil. Jesus put His foot on the devil's head and took the keys of death and hell from his hand. (Rev 1:18.) When it looks to my children like everything is upside-down and backwards, it's time for me to cheer them on. That's my job.

Let's look now at the special gifts we are to use in serving one another as a good steward of God's grace.

9

Your Child's Gift From God

I want to talk to you now about gifts that are given to us by God. We will be looking at several Scripture references.

Let's read from 1 Peter 4, taken from the *New American Standard Bible*:

1 Peter 4:10 NAS — **As each one has received a special gift, employ it in serving one another, as good stewards of the manifold grace of God.**

Next, let's go to Romans 12, reading from *The Amplified Bible*:

Romans 12:6-8 AMP — **Having gifts (faculties, talents, qualities) that differ according to the grace given us, let us use them: [He whose gift is] prophecy, [let him prophesy] according to the proportion of his faith;**

[He whose gift is] practical service, let him give himself to serving; he who teaches, to his teaching;

He who exhorts (encourages), to his exhortation; he who contributes, let him do it in simplicity and liberality; he who gives aid and superintends, with zeal and singleness of mind; he who does acts of mercy, with genuine cheerfulness and joyful eagerness.

Then, looking again in 1 Peter 4, from the *New American Standard Bible*, it says:

As each one has received a special gift, employ it in serving one another, as good stewards of the manifold grace of God.

Whoever speaks, let him speak, as it were, the utterances of God; whoever serves, let him do so as by the strength which God supplies; so that in all things God may be glorified through Jesus Christ, to whom belongs the glory and dominion forever and ever. Amen (vv. 10,11 NAS).

Speakers and Servers

At the moment of conception every person was gifted by God to do certain things. Basically, people are divided into two groups, either *speakers* or *servers*.

The world classifies children into two categories: *high achievers* and *thinkers*. These secular terms are used in college testing.

So, every person, whether adult or child, will go into one of these two categories: *speakers* or *servers*.

Speakers are those people who like to talk. According to Romans 12, they operate in the gifts of prophecy, teaching, exhorting and administration.

People with the other three gifts — serving, giving and compassion — are the doers; they like to help other people. Kids who have these gifts just can't pass by without helping somebody, and they are the ones always bringing home stray animals. This is a gift of God, a grace gift given at the moment of conception.

Psalm 139 in *The Amplified Bible* says this:

For You did form my inward parts; You did knit me together in my mother's womb.

I will confess and praise You for You are fearful and wonderful and for the awful wonder of my birth! Wonderful are Your works, and that my inner self knows right well.

My frame was not hidden from You when I was being formed in secret [and] intricately and curiously wrought [as if embroidered with various colors] in the depths of the earth [a region of darkness and mystery].

Your eyes saw my unformed substance, and in Your book all the days [of my life] were written before ever they took shape, when as yet there was none of them (vv. 13-16).

Abilities Are From God

These gifts, talents and abilities are from God, but what we do with them is our responsibility.

While attending a school awards banquet, I watched as a student walked across the platform to receive a scholarship to a four-year university which several other students had hoped to win. I commented to the principal the mixed emotions I had about that student winning the scholarship. He replied by telling me what a high grade-point average the student had.

"That may be true," I replied, "but there are several other students just as deserving, if not more so."

I have known both young students and older adults who have gifts which they ride through life but never fully steward. Yet there are others with fewer abilities who give maximum effort. Some children can make an A in a subject without much effort, while others may have to study three hours every night to make that same A. It isn't how many gifts we have but what we do with those gifts that's important to God. To whom much is given, much is required. (Luke 12:48.)

We humans judge differently from how God judges, don't we? But He gives everyone severally, according to his ability. Each of us has a different ability.

I was attending an athletics banquet when awards were given out. The biggest trophy was the rebounding trophy. When the kid came up to receive it, I remember commenting to the coach how that athlete may have gotten the most rebounds that year but other players were more dedicated. I said:

"This particular player would show up late at practice; and he didn't work very hard during the line drills because he knew he was so good. Why should we be giving this kid a trophy for jumping two feet off the ground if God gifted him to jump that high? I know another kid who could jump only a few inches off the ground when he first got here, but now he jumps much higher — and we aren't giving him a thing!"

Don't Try To Be Like Somebody Else

Children sometimes would get their eyes on somebody else. One young elementary student has said to me, "Mr. McGee, I read my Bible and I pray and I go to church, but I didn't make the baseball team like they did."

I said: "Son, the reason you didn't is because you can't hit the baseball. Some who made the team don't go to church or read their Bible or pray, but they were born with something called eye-hand coordination. You could make the team, but you will need to spend a few hours each week in the batting cage."

Here is what we all need to understand: The Bible says, **The gifts and calling of God are without repentance** (Rom. 11:29). As mentioned before, these gifts are given at the moment of conception. You may live your entire life and never serve God with your gift, but He will never take that gift from you.

A man's gift will make room for him, and money for him too. That's why some people can make millions of dollars by singing great songs or by investing lots of money on Wall Street and curse God all the way to their grave. Their talent and their ability are

144

gifts from God. Good stewardship of your gift may prosper you but it will not take you to heaven.

If we don't explain that to our children, all their lives they will try to be like somebody else.

I am talking to you about the gifts so that you can teach your kids. Let's quit frustrating our children by wanting them to be like other children; they can't do it. We have to find out what our children are good at and not push them to be like someone else. My child can go out and practice baseball from now until the sun goes down and never be as good as a professional like baseball great Ted Williams, for instance.

Ted Williams had a specific gift from God of eye-hand coordination most people never have, and never will have. But Ted can serve as an inspiration to my children to be the absolute best they can be.

Other players have had that eye-hand coordination. They could go out on the town one night, get drunk until their belly hung over their belt, fornicate, curse God, then come into the ballpark the next day and hit home runs. They didn't need to practice; they could just slap baseballs over the fence.

In basketball, whether college or high school, any point guard who is quick on the court will normally not be a great cross-country runner. There are two kinds of muscles in athletics: a quick-twitch muscle and an elongated muscle.

The runner with a quick-twitch muscle can win a 100-yard dash but not do well in a long-distance run. He can't last that long because he doesn't have endurance. His muscles are quick, but he can't compete in the long haul.

Another kid who is slow on the court can run five miles and not even be breathing hard. He will beat the others every time because he has a different kind of muscle. That's a gift.

Now as we have read from Romans 12, there are seven different gifts. Every child falls into one of these seven categories and will have a bent toward that gift. But it's important to be sure that our children are seeking the right gift — the one God meant for them to have.

A Dad Trying To Make His Son Follow in His Footsteps

One man whom I knew desired earnestly that his son follow in his footsteps. He was an engineer, and all he wanted was for his son to be an engineer too. But his son couldn't make it through algebra. I kept telling the dad that his son may never be an engineer, but he was convinced that he would.

You need to realize, Mom and Dad, that gifts don't get passed down. They are not hereditary. I know that's a misconception according to the world, but it's still true: Gifts aren't passed down!

That boy was flunking algebra, and that made him ineligible for basketball. Then he couldn't be with his buddies on the team, so he got really frustrated and started hanging around kids who didn't do anything. He was miserable, and his mom and dad were miserable. But the dad was still determined that his son would be an engineer.

Finally, we had a conference about it. I said: "Dad, your son will never be an engineer. And even if he became one, I would never drive across a bridge or get into an elevator he had built. Math is a major struggle for him. But he really has the gift of gab. He's quick-witted and runs his mouth continuously, so he would make a great preacher, politician or salesman. He will do something using his mouth, but he will never build any bridges. You need to start finding out how to enhance his gift so that he can do what he's good at."

Now a gift is a tool from God; but if left unchallenged, it will just wither away. You have to steward it. So find out what your child is good at, praise him for it and then start stewarding what he has by taking him places and exposing him to people with a similar gift.

My Two Oldest Daughters and Their Gifts

I will use my two oldest daughters, Sarah and Jessica, as examples of the gifts.

As a school administrator I have had an inside track to many of the tests, both secular and Christian, that show the personality gifts our kids are leaning toward. I gave these tests to my children when they were younger. Sarah's main forte was as an administrator while Jessica was an exhorter.

Both girls played on the high-school basketball team. Sarah was involved in student government and Jessica was on the cheerleading squad. They each had a different bent. On the basketball court Sarah and Jessica were the opposite.

Jessica is left-handed, and she was a great little three-point shooter. Her junior year in high school, she won the three-point shooting title at the Oklahoma All-State Festival. She was quick with her hands, which made her great at stealing the basketball, and several times she won top defensive honors.

Now Sarah was not the most talented basketball player on the team. One coach said of her: "This kid is the most intelligent player we have. The problem is, she can't dribble from one end of the court to the other without losing the ball. But she's getting better."

However, Sarah was a big contributor to the team, earning respect from the other players. She knew what was going on around her. She was the best at passing the ball of any I had ever seen on the court; then when inside the paint, she was close enough to do her thing and was a great player.

Being administrative-minded, Sarah organized and kept everything put in order. Her notebooks were kept very neat with tabs dividing the subjects. She couldn't do her homework unless things were immaculate in her room. Then once they were, she would go to work.

Before leaving the house, Sarah would stand in front of the mirror for what seemed like hours, getting everything in proper order. She wore makeup and a nice outfit, with pocketbook to match.

Jessica, on the other hand, could shove a bobby pin in her hair and just throw on a sweat suit before going out the door.

Because Jessica is an exhorter, people like being around her; she has the ability to make everybody laugh and feel good.

Now when it came to money, Sarah knew exactly how much she had in savings and exactly how much to give in church — 10 percent, not 10.1 percent. When we went on vacation, she had saved up her money and knew exactly how much she could spend.

Jessica, on the other hand, wasn't much on saving money, because she was a real giver. Remember the gift of compassion? You could ask her, "How much money do you have?" She would answer, "I don't know; I gave it all away." She wouldn't have any money, but she would have all kinds of things. She would get more things given to her than any child I have ever seen. That's because she is a giver.

Sarah lives life and she loves every minute of it. Her attitude is, "If I have to be somewhere, I might as well be in charge" (administrative bent), whereas Jessica doesn't care who's in charge; she just wants to have a good time (exhortive bent).

Jessica doesn't seem to worry about anything; there is no place in her brain for worry, so things don't clutter her mind. Everybody seems to love her. She just likes being there for people.

The point I am making is this: both Sarah and Jessica have their needs met through two entirely different means; each of them is bent in a different direction.

So, giftings are different and every child is gifted. Remember, these gifts are without repentance. God will never pull them from anybody; they are His gifts to us.

Don't Use Gifts As an Excuse

While I want my children to know their gifts so that they can begin to steward them and to fulfill God's plan for their lives, I don't want them to use their gifts as a cop-out and not do things simply because they aren't good at them. As a matter of fact, the opposite is true.

I remember years ago when I was working in management in the electrical manufacturing industry I attended an in-service workshop one weekend. The instructor gave a talk that has always stayed with me. He said that every individual's job is divided into three parts:

1. One-third of our job is the part we are very good at and love to do, and we receive many praises when we do it.

2. One-third of our job is the part we are qualified to do and will do when required.

3. But one-third of every person's job is the part we aren't good at and don't like to do. When we try, we usually receive some criticism, so we avoid it at every opportunity.

Yet, the success we realize on our jobs, regardless of our vocation, depends on how much time we give to the one-third we are not good at.

So, while we have our children focus on the area in which God has gifted them, there is no excuse for them to avoid those areas of life that aren't much fun.

Helping Our Kids To Make the Right Choice

As parents, we need to find out what our children are good at and start trying to narrow down their choices as they go through life.

When we gave a vocational test to our kids, we came up with about twelve careers that each of them would be good at. They each are probably going to follow one of those twelve vocations. Now that's not "Thus saith the Lord." It's just the results of a test, but there is some wisdom attached to it. As the kids have gotten older, they have narrowed it down to a handful of possible vocations.

Going into her senior year of high school, Sarah narrowed it down to two areas she might like to pursue. When we were getting ready to go on vacation, she would say, "Hey, Dad, there's a certain kind of school down there. Can we stop in?"

I have a good idea about the direction she will eventually go; I have just always bragged on how good she was. She is so sharp that you won't ever win an argument with her. She would have all the facts nailed down, so she would make a great teacher. Now that's the last thing she thought she would want to be; but unless God leads her in some other direction, I will keep feeding the gift until she does one of two things: either consumes it and stewards it, or chokes on it. If she chokes on it, she will spit it out and say, "Dad, that's one thing I know I don't want to do!"

Sometimes our kids have to first find out what they don't want to do. So many times, because of the way our society is, kids are faced with too many options.

Wasn't it wonderful when we used to go into the ice cream store and have a choice of only three flavors, either chocolate, vanilla or strawberry? Then Baskin-Robbins came along and confused everybody. Long lines developed at the counter as people were trying to decide which of those thirty-one flavors they wanted. Then along came nearly as many toppings. You almost need an algebraic equation just to order some ice cream. Then as you walk out the door, the thought hits you, *You know, I really wanted that other flavor.*

It's like life has just gotten too complicated. There are too many options. What we parents have to do is to help narrow down those choices in our kids' minds. Then when they get down to it, they will know what to do.

With that in mind, as parents we need to understand our own gifts and callings; then we can be the cheerleader for our kids. They are gifted to do something; and, with God's help, we can help them find out what it is.

There are several good books on this subject that can be found in Christian bookstores, secular bookstores and educational stores. Do some investigating and then test your kids. There are even tests for preschoolers that take only about fifteen minutes. All you have to do is give the test and look at the answers. You will probably say, "That's about what I thought." That's what parents usually find out.

These tests will normally confirm things you already knew. They can help your children in junior high and high school to start narrowing down what they are good at and head them in the right direction. When you find something they like to do, then you can promote it by exposing them to it. This will cost you some time; but, I promise you, it will pay great dividends.

One of the best books to start with would be *Discover Your Children's Gifts* by Don and Katie Fortune.[1]

Let's go now into the subject of your child's handling of his money.

---

[1] (GRAND RAPIDS: FLEMING H. REVELL, 1989).

10

Your Child's Money

Another principle we must teach our children is how to handle money.

It seems that in this country we have been fed a lie about wealth. For some reason, we have been told that all those rich people got that way by some illegal means. Some people say, "What we should do is take all that money away from the rich people and give it to the poor people; that will make everything right."

If all the money was taken away from the wealthy in this country, in five years most of them would have it back.

As God says in His Word:

Proverbs 10:4 — **...the hand of the diligent maketh rich.**

Most wealthy people got that way by working for it. That's how you get wealth, and this can be a real shocker to some people. After watching so much television, they think all rich people are like those scoundrels on TV who got it by doing wrong.

If you think that way, you need to read your Bible. It says those who are hasty to get rich will lose it. (See Prov. 28:22.) Either God is a liar or He is telling the truth. (I know which one describes *my* God!)

I like to read about successful people who get things done. You might be surprised at how many of them are born-again Christians, and some don't even have college degrees.

One of my favorite books is *Student's Gold*, which is published by Honor Books in Tulsa, Oklahoma. This book is a must for every parent who has a child in school. My favorite chapter is called "The Failure's Hall of Fame," which lists several famous people in history and how many times they failed before succeeding. Diligence was the common bond among them.

One time I was reading in a secular magazine about some of the top businesses in our country. It told about one man's business that services restaurants in the airports and provides food on airplanes. But that was only one of about seventeen companies he owns. He once worked as a bellhop in an Oklahoma City hotel. He doesn't have a college degree, but he is a successful businessman.

In the article, this businessman gave the top priorities in his life: number one was God, number two was his family and number three was his job. He supports missionaries and churches and gives away money. This man is a success because he puts God first place in his life.

Some people have said, "Rich people are mean, ugly, evil and full of the devil!" Well, if they're really so bad, why is it that everyone is trying so hard to be like them by getting money? Why don't we just quit working, go home, sit down and prop up our feet?

The Importance of a Budget

Did you know that the majority of Americans have no budget?

If you are without a budget, that means you don't know the "state of your flocks." As Proverbs 27:23 says, **Be thou diligent to know the state of thy flocks, and look well to thy herds.** If you don't know the state of your flocks, you can lose what you have.

During a counseling session, I have often asked that person, "Do you have a budget?"

The answer so many times has been: "No. I don't have any money to budget. But when I get some, then I'll start one."

"If you don't budget now," I say, "you won't ever have any money. By finding out how much trouble you're in, then we will know what to believe God for."

This can be an eye-opener. I remember the first time my wife and I went through this. We were thousands of dollars in debt, and I was depressed — with a capital D! *How did we get there?* A little at a time. Without a budget, we had no idea where our money was going. We might have made a good salary each month, but we were spending every bit of it; we had also fallen into a habit of using credit cards.

This world system is designed by Satan to put us under — to steal, kill and destroy. (John 10:10.) If we don't realize this, we will be ignorant of the devil's devices and he will take us in.

Kids Must Be Taught About Money

We have to teach our children how to handle their money. Let me give you an example.

I used to always be faced with the chore of going to the grocery store with the wife and children. With a family as big as mine, I am a two-cart shopper. When I showed up there, the grocer, who knew me on a first-name basis, would walk with me down the first aisle and we would visit.

Grocery stores are designed in certain ways. It seems that the first area we came to was the bakery, and I would start hearing from my kids: "Daddy, can we have a donut?"

"No, we don't need any donuts today. Keep moving."

By going through a grocery store, I have discovered where hell can be found on earth: it's the cereal aisle of that store. Do you ever go down that aisle? If so, you know what I mean.

Through the years, I have noticed how that area has expanded. At one time those cereals fit on half of one aisle; now they go all the way down both sides. There is every kind of cereal imaginable. Wheat, rice and oats are all crammed into different shapes and sizes and can be found in various colors.

One of my kids would pick up a box of cereal and say, "Dad, can we buy this one?"

After looking at it, I would say, "Five dollars and eighty-three cents! And we wouldn't get eight bowls of cereal out of that! Put it back on the shelf and get the oatmeal!"

When we had made it all the way through the grocery store, I would go to the check-out stand and write a check for more than two hundred dollars for those two carts filled with groceries. Then all the way home my kids would be crying because they didn't get what they wanted.

When the kids were a little older, I was buying more than three baskets of groceries. They would eat everything they could get their hands on. I actually reached the point where I had to put locks on the pantry. I locked up everything except the refrigerator; and I have said that I would eventually do that.

Finally, I reached a certain point with the kids. I got mad the way husbands do sometimes and I told my wife: "I'm never taking the children to the grocery store again — never! You can go by yourself or I'll go by myself, but we will never go as a family again. This just isn't a family function."

I knew that attitude wasn't from God, so I decided to give the children their own money. Now that was a real challenge!

Allowances

I had to come up with answers to questions like: How much do I give them, and what are they being paid for? (Now don't ask me how much allowance you should give your kids; that's between you and your pocketbook.)

Allowances are given to our kids almost gratuitously. But there were times when we had no money for allowances, so we gave our kids little gold stars. In effect we were saying, "That's like an IOU. We'll pay you someday."

Now there are certain chores my kids do at home that they don't get paid for. If they wear clothes, they launder them. If they eat off a dish, they wash it. If they use the toilet, they clean it. These are just normal household duties.

There is money kids can earn and money they can save. When my kids got their own money, we set up bank accounts in their own names.

I remember when they first got their own money. The next time we went to the grocery store, Corrie said, "Daddy, can I have a donut?"

"Sure, honey. Do you have your own money?"

"No, Dad."

"Well, honey, the Bible says I could lend but you aren't supposed to borrow, so I can't give you any." Then we walked on through the store.

Now that may sound cruel, but it's the truth.

A couple of weeks later we went back to the grocery store, but this time Corrie remembered to take her own money (and she never forgot it again). She said, "Daddy, can I have a donut?"

"Do you have your own money?"

"Yes, sir, I have it right here," and she held out a little red pouch.

"Go ahead, honey. I'll meet you at the check-out counter."

About an hour later as I was checking out, Corrie came up to me, and I said, "Honey, where's your white bakery sack?"

"I don't have it."

"Have you eaten it already?"

"No, sir."

"Well, where's your donut?"

"I didn't buy one."

"Why not?"

"Too expensive."

If I had known that would happen, I could have saved thousands of dollars years ago. I found out that kids will spend their parents' money all day long — but not their own! They will squeeze a nickel until it bleeds.

So if you want to save some money, just give your kids their own money. What you give away, you will get back; what you hold on to, you will lose.

Giving

At one time we lived in an area of Missouri where farmers planted thousands of acres of corn. For them to produce a big crop, they had to determine how much seed to put in the ground.

If you want a little crop of eating corn for the table, just plant two or three rows. But if you plan to sell your crop and use its profit to make house payments, you had better pull the tractor out of the barn. You can't just take a little pack of seeds, shove them in the ground and say, "We're just believing for a big return, so we need a miracle, God."

As it says in the Bible, God gives seed to the sower. (Isa. 55:10; 2 Cor. 9:10.) I have tried to teach my children when they are young that they are to be givers.

What we plant, we will reap. If we plant little, we will reap little; if we plant much, we will reap much. Even unbelievers know this. Unfortunately, many Christians don't understand it.

The inclination of our sin nature is to hold on to things, always using words like *me, I, my, want, keep* and *hoard*. With an attitude like this, we would never have a thing. The only way we can beat this world system and the devil is by getting on God's financial plan, which is a plan of giving. Once we hit that path, there is nothing that can stop God from giving back to us.

We are responsible to plant this truth into our children. If we don't, when they grow up, they will stay in debt all of their lives. They will be struggling to always make ends meet. They will be using an old, broken frying pan and driving a beat-up old car. They never will have anything without a knowledge of the truth. They have to go to work — which is a part of it — but they also have to start giving. These two principles of working and giving have to be used together.

In Psalm 112:1-3 we are told that parents who fear the Lord and delight greatly in His commandments will see their children grow up to be mighty on this planet, that *wealth and riches* will be in their house and their righteousness (or right doing) will endure forever.

The earlier we start teaching these principles to our kids the better. God will honor the faith of a child.

I have seen my daughter, Jessica, get things, and it just blows me away. Why does this happen with Jessica? Because she is a giver. I have watched her. She doesn't think a thing about it; she just does it with a pure heart and loves doing it. Seeing that, I think, *Dear Lord, give me convictions like that.*

Galatians 6:7 — **Be not deceived; God is not mocked: for whatsoever a man soweth, that shall he also reap.**

This is God's law, and it's a law that we must put into our children. If they are to be carrying on the work of God, they can't do it if they are completely broke. They must get their needs met and then have enough to give to others.

The Bible says, **Feed the flock of God...** (1 Peter 5:2). We can't be of help to the flock of God when we are broke. First, our needs have to be met; then we will be able to help feed the flock of God.

Savings

Now regarding money, savings is a big thing in our family. Proverbs 3:10 says, **So shall thy barns be filled with plenty....** Our "barn" is like our savings account. I have told my kids that, if they don't spend all of the money given to them in their allowance, I will take whatever amount they have left at the end of the month and match it dollar for dollar.

My kids are allowed to get into their savings accounts only twice a year: when we go on vacation in the summer and at Christmas time. At these times, they can take out all but one hundred dollars. That one hundred dollars stays in, because that's the original amount I used to open their accounts.

Sometimes my kids will say something like: "Gee, Dad, I saw this *great* sale! It's seventy-five percent off! Just let me take some from my savings account. I promise that I'll put it right back in!"

"No way! Forget it!" I say.

That's one way I work at teaching their flesh.

I know about this because I went through it myself. I used to spend every penny that I had. If something was on sale, I bought it. That's how I got so deeply in debt. I always got what I wanted; but then when it wore out, I was still paying for it. It's a sick feeling to still be paying for something that's already been thrown in the trash can.

I didn't feel too smart about what I had done, and I don't want my kids to ever have to go through that. Of course, there are things our kids will have to learn on their own, but there are principles we can put to work in them.

Let's go now into the topic of teaching your children about work.

11

Teaching Your Child About Work

Now I want us to look into the subject of teaching our kids about work, about doing chores at home. What should we have them doing around the house?

There are two words in the Bible every parent should be familiar with: *work* and *diligent.*

Work

Proverbs 18:9 — **He also that is slothful in his *work* is brother to him that is a great waster.**

2 Thessalonians 3:10-12 — **For even when we were with you, this we commanded you, that if any would not *work*, neither should he eat. For we hear that there are some which walk among you disorderly, *working not* at all, but are busybodies. Now them that are such we command and exhort by our Lord Jesus Christ, that with quietness they *work*, and eat their own bread.**

Diligent

Proverbs 10:4 — **He becometh poor that dealeth with a slack hand: but the hand of the *diligent* maketh rich.**

Proverbs 12:24 — **The hand of the *diligent* shall bear rule: but the slothful shall be under tribute.**

Proverbs 12:27 — **The slothful man roasteth not that which he took in hunting: but the substance of a *diligent* man is precious.**

> Proverbs 13:4 — The soul of the sluggard desireth, and hath nothing: but the soul of the *diligent* shall be made fat.

> Proverbs 21:5 — The thoughts of the *diligent* tend only to plenteousness; but of every one that is hasty only to want.

> Proverbs 22:29 — Seest thou a man *diligent* in his business? he shall stand before kings; he shall not stand before mean men.

Work is part of God's plan for our lives, and God says there are great rewards for those who are diligent in their work. Good work habits begin in the home.

Jobs My Kids Do at Home

Let me tell you, there are lots of jobs my kids are involved in around our house. For instance, I remember when my son was only four years old he could make his own bed. He didn't do a very good job of it, but he still did it, and was thrilled to do it. I encouraged him every chance I got. Of course, it didn't stay that way long; in an hour his whole bedroom was torn to pieces and looked like a tornado had gone through twice — going through once, then backing up and going through again!

So don't get any perfect images of life around our house. There will be days when everything looks wonderful and other days when it looks like a riot had hit the night before. It's up to me, the parent, to set some standards for my children.

I tell all of my children: "You owe me forty-five minutes of manual labor per day. I don't care when you give it to me; it could be at four in the morning for all I care."

Then every Saturday, they owe me two hours of manual labor. I have a list of things that need to be done around the house. I don't care when they do them, whether it's eight o'clock in the morning or ten o'clock at night.

Now when Tessa was six she could run the vacuum cleaner; though not as well as her mom or me, she hit the high spots and did a good job. Mom and I have other things we need to be doing, like taking care of six kids while running the household and the ministry at the same time. All of us have chores to do around the house, so everybody has to pull their own load.

Our Home Is a Blessing

Usually, Friday night is family night at our house. I normally fly out on Saturday mornings when going off to hold seminars, so we don't do any chores on Friday night; we do "family things."

Home is a fun place for us, and people like to come over and visit. Our freezer is full of junk food, and we have lots of playthings around the house, like basketball goals, volleyball nets, Nintendo games, videos and bicycles. You name it — we have it. We even have a big above-ground swimming pool in the backyard that I found at a great price. I have learned that you can get some really good bargains if you will look for them.

Our house is located way out in the country on two-and-a-half acres at the back of a mountain. It's a great place to live!

At one time we lived in an older small house, measuring nine hundred square feet, with carpet that had big chunks out of it. It was all we could afford at that time, but I was believing God for something better. Success doesn't come overnight; it comes with time. It won't just be dumped on you or brought down the chimney by Santa Claus; it comes by working, by believing God and by setting your goals.

I remember when my oldest child was five years old she was singing in her bedroom one night, making up little songs, and she began prophesying about where we were going to live. She just began singing, without really knowing what she was doing. Sometimes kids can make up silly-sounding little songs; but then all of a sudden she began describing a house. It was exactly like the house we are living in now.

But our home wasn't just dropped out of an airplane. It took four years of saving, two years of planning and then almost a year to be physically built. It took work — and lots of it!

But it's what we wanted. Some people might think it a strange place to live, but we love it. And it's our home! But it didn't just happen. We didn't receive a check in the mail to pay for it.

Our children saw us put this principle of working and trusting God into operation.

In Proverbs 16, verse 3, we read: **Commit thy *works* unto the Lord, and thy *thoughts* shall be established.** Verse 9 says, **A man's heart deviseth his way: but the Lord directeth his steps.**

A principle in the Word of God tells us that, when we do something, God does something. We walk around the walls, and God knocks them down. We lift up the staff, and He parts the waters. We make the mud, and He opens the eyes.

As we see here in Proverbs 16, there are four steps in this process:

verse 3:   (1)   We commit our works (prayer) — Something we do.

                 (2)   God establishes our thoughts — Something God does.

verse 9:   (3)   Man devises his way (makes plans) — Something we do.

                 (4)   God orders steps — Something God does.

If I pray about a situation, God will give me thoughts to think. With those thoughts, I write down my plans. As I walk out those plans, the Lord orders my steps.

For us to accomplish God's plan for our lives will take work, and I am helping my children to reach God's best for them by teaching them work habits at home.

Jeremiah 29:11, NIV — **"For I know the plans I have for you," declares the Lord, "plans to prosper you and not to harm you, plans to give you hope and a future."**

God plans for us to prosper. We flow with Him by working and being diligent.

These days it seems kids are always saying, "I want it — and I want it now!" The Bible teaches that man should work and work diligently. The basic law of sowing and reaping that is taught all through the Bible is involved here. In order to harvest, we must plant. So we need to teach our kids how to work while they are still at home and how to enjoy the fruits of their labor.

That's why when lots of children grow up and get married, they can't even boil water. They were never allowed in the kitchen because their parents didn't want them to make a mess. But they can't learn if they aren't taught, even though they will make a mess until they do learn.

When you have kids in the house, there is going to be a mess somewhere. We seem to be constantly patching up something around our place. We have had to replace closet doors because of big holes which just suddenly appeared. It seems kids can break anything.

Adjustments Must Be Made

Sometimes we have to go four or five days without doing any work around our house. Basketball season is one of those times, starting in December and running through February.

During these days our house looks as if three tornadoes had just camped out there. When it's time to eat, we have to first wash a dish. When we need something to wear, we have to go through all the piles of clothes and pick out something.

Sometimes when I teach people these principles of parenting, they think my house must be an immaculate place in which to live. But that just isn't true. With all the kids around our house, it's a regular place.

But what we have — and what you need to have — is a standard. Our children know when we get five days behind on chores. They know that, when Saturday comes, they owe me two hours of manual labor and they know there is plenty of work to do. So it's an all-out effort, and they will work together.

Sometimes we have to stand around and tell them what to do, step by step, one thing at a time. I say, "Now I want you to pick this up and carry it right over there." But everything gets done.

Keep a Schedule

When it comes to chores, you need to have a list. Make a job description for each child, showing a list of things he or she is to do, and stick it on the refrigerator. Then put a check mark by each job as it gets done.

But remember this: even if your child did a great job yesterday, the natural tendency is for him to be lazy tomorrow. He will just want to eat and sleep. That's the sin nature. He will never want to do anything if he has no goal to reach for.

So you might want to get a little daytimer that your kid can use for keeping a schedule. I try to keep an updated social calendar for all my children, so I know where they are even before they do. It may sound a little complicated, but it seems to work well.

There are things you can do to help your child get his life planned out and give it some structure. Life isn't perfect and can be pure chaos at times. All kinds of things which you don't have scheduled can happen; but without a plan, you won't know how to recover. You may get hit with a tidal wave, but you can't just lie there and rest; you have to get up and start moving. You have to recoup and get back to doing what you had planned to do.

When Under Pressure

As an example, Denise and I were getting ready to leave to hold a marriage seminar in San Antonio, Texas. I had just come home from St. Louis, where I had held three meetings back to back. When I came home, my five favorite white shirts needed to be laundered, but I had forgotten it. I had even written a reminder in my daytimer: "Put shirts in laundry." But I didn't read it.

On the morning we were to leave town, we woke up at five o'clock and were busy getting ready to go when all of a sudden I remembered those shirts. So I quickly threw them in the washing machine. Then after changing them to the dryer, I plugged up two irons. Denise was going to iron some of them while Sarah ironed the others.

Then while I was packing up boxes for the trip, I suddenly heard Denise's voice, and the sound I heard wasn't good. It seems one of the girls had borrowed a dark, navy-blue headband, and it had been thrown in the washer with my white shirts. As a result, my favorite white shirts had taken on that acid-rain look.

We had to be at the airport in thirty-five minutes. *What was I to do?*

Sarah said, "Dad, you're off schedule."

My response to her was simply: "Just go out and get in the Suburban!"

As we were driving to the airport, Denise said, "What are we going to do?"

"I don't know," I said. "Let's just drive and I'll think a minute." I thought, *What am I going to do about shirts? I can't show up in those hippie-looking shirts.*

Then as we were driving by the shopping mall, I suddenly said, "There's Dillard's! I'll just go in and buy five new shirts." So we stopped and I ran inside. I said to the salesman, "I need five shirts!" Then I grabbed up the shirts and wrote out a check.

By the time we had made it to the airport, not only had we missed our plane, but I had gotten a speeding ticket on the way.

Standing there, Sarah was watching me under pressure. She said, "Daddy, you missed your plane. What are you going to do?"

"Well, honey, there are lots of airplanes. Another one will be flying out sometime. We'll just find one going somewhere, and we'll get there."

And we did. It was just thirty minutes before the meeting started when we landed, and I had to change clothes in the airport, but we made it on time to the meeting.

"Don't Waste Money!"

Sometimes when I am trying to teach my kids about work, I get onto them about wasting money. Do you ever do that? It really upsets me. I am always reminding them, "Don't waste money!" Speaking of some particular situation, I will say, "Do you know how much money that cost us?" Then I go into a long dissertation.

That's why the Bible says those three things in Micah 6:8, which we read earlier in our study. Again, this verse says:

> ...what doth the Lord require of thee, but *to do justly,* and *to love mercy,* and *to walk humbly with thy God?*

Sometimes the very thing you get onto your kids about is the very thing you make the mistake of doing yourself.

Let me give you an example of how we can react to certain situations.

I remember when I had really been getting onto my kids about money. I had just finished working on the annual family budget and was becoming like a broken record. I kept saying, "Do you know how much money that cost us?" I would be nice sometimes and we would laugh, but other times I would get really tough with them.

The previous fall I had bought two bales of hay to spread on the ground so that the grass would grow between all the huge rocks that lay around our property. One of those bales had been left sitting out all winter until green grass was starting to grow out the top of it.

Denise reminded me of it, saying, "Are you going to do something with that bale of hay on the back hill behind the house? I'd appreciate it if you would get it out of the backyard."

"Okay, hon," I said. "Don't worry about it."

I went outside and was going to pick up that bale and move it, but the wires had rusted, and they broke. So then that big, wet bale of hay was just laying there. What was I going to do then?

I decided to get the wheelbarrow out of the shed, but I saw that its tire had gone flat. So I got our pickup truck and loaded the bale into the back of it.

As I was driving around to the front of the house, Denise came out onto the deck and said, "Where are you going?"

"I'm going to back the truck down the hill beside the house and push the hay into the ravine." I thought that would be good for the creek.

"Don't you get stuck," she said.

So I backed up to the ravine and pushed that hay over the edge. I didn't get stuck, even though it had been raining; I stayed right on top of the ground, and that hay just rolled down into the ravine. Then all of that was taken care of.

But when I started to drive the truck forward, it wouldn't go. Its rear tires turned, but it wasn't moving. Then it started to sink.

Soon, all the kids were out on the deck with Denise, leaning over the rail and looking down at me. I could see Denise's mouth moving, as if she were saying, "I told him so! I told him so!"

As I kept working at it, I was getting madder by the minute.

Finally, I said to Denise, "Go get the Suburban and drive it down here!" Then I got a big chain and hooked it to the truck. I said to her, "I'll get that truck out — you just sit behind the wheel and steer it."

I started pushing on the gas in the Suburban and pulling the chain. But then that chain just broke apart!

By this time I was really upset and was covered with sweat. Then it started to rain.

The kids on the deck were saying, "Daddy, can you get it out?"

"No, I can't! Get in the house!" I yelled back.

As it turned out, we had to call a wrecker to come and pull out that truck. Since we live way out in the country, we don't have wreckers right down the road, so that cost me ninety dollars!

When the wrecker came, I was at work, so Denise called to tell me about it. She said, "He got the truck out and it cost us ninety dollars, but that's not all."

"What else?" I asked.

"He says you wore out your pressure plate and clutch trying to pull it out of the mud."

"Oh, he doesn't know what he's talking about!" I said. "It can't be ruined; I wasn't doing it that long."

But when I got home, I found out that, sure enough, the truck was shot. No pressure plate. No clutch. It wouldn't move. The engine just made a loud noise.

We really needed that truck, so what were we going to do? Then I said, "I'll call the wrecker and have him to come out and tow it in." Well, that cost me another ninety dollars!

It seems that one bale of hay, which had originally cost two dollars, wound up costing me $424.13!

When I drove the truck home after it was repaired, Sarah and Jessica were on the deck waiting for me. They were looking at one another and just laughing. "Hey, Dad, how much was it?"

"It was enough," I said. "I could have bought a whole barn full of hay for what I've done."

About the time you accuse your kids of doing something, you will wind up doing it yourself. So you have to understand that you are setting an example for them. They are watching you, so they won't be any better stewards over things than you are.

I learned a good lesson through that whole situation. I found out that I still know how to do dumb things.

That's why you need to always be humble whenever you are making rules and regulations for your kids.

Example of a Worker Who Has Vision

Now, I want to share a story about work. While I was working for an electrical wiring cable company, it was my job to hire and train people in manufacturing. We hired young guys right out of high school.

This may be the most important point you get from this study: Most young men don't know where they want to go in life; they just know they want a job. Being right out of high school, it's time for them to go to work.

When starting to work for our company, those guys were paid a good hourly rate, about two dollars an hour more than they could make anywhere else in town. So they were proud to work there, even though it was hard manual labor.

I remember when these guys came in to apply for a job. Some had their shirttails hanging out; some had their shirts unbuttoned down to their bellies, with their sleeves cut off; and some were dipping snuff. I had them to fill out an application, then I talked with them.

With all of those guys sitting there, another young man named Mark walked in. He had just graduated from high school as those other boys had, only he looked different: he was wearing a white shirt and tie.

He looked different, and he acted different. It seems that his dad worked at a local factory; but as a born-again Christian, he was planting the vision inside his kids that God had something good for them.

When Mark came in, he said, "I'd like a job."

After asking his name, I said, "Oh, I don't think we have any jobs you would be looking for."

"I'm looking for any job, even janitor," he said. "I don't care what the job is. I need a job, and I hear you have an opening."

"We do, but you won't be wearing a shirt and tie on this job, son. This is hard manual labor. It's going to be dirty and greasy."

"I understand that, sir, and I appreciate it. Can I ask you a question? How much money will I be making five years from now?"

"Son, I don't know how much money _I'll_ be making five years from now."

"Well, I just thought I'd like to know if you had a graduated pay scale or what the benefits were."

Then I said, "I'll get you a booklet so that you'll know."

I wound up hiring that young man, and as it turned out, he was a great worker. He showed up early and stayed late, and within eight months was made lead foreman.

Our workers were given two ten-minute breaks on the job, and most of the guys working the big welders would be watching the clock: _3...2...1...BREAK!_ Then all of them took a break; and when the break was over, those guys would hang around for another two or three minutes, trying to stretch it out. Those guys didn't have much vision for life.

Mark, on the other hand, hardly ever took a break. He worked through his breaks to get ahead. The other guys didn't like him taking a break anyhow because, when he did, he would witness to them. They didn't want that, so they just let him keep working.

A year later there developed the need for a junior salesman in the front office, so the bosses came to me and said, "We'd like to talk to that kid over there," pointing at Mark. After that, he was moved into the front office.

Before long, after hours, Mark was spending his own time, selling items that had been thrown into the trash bin because we couldn't make a good-enough profit on them. They were by-products of goods we were producing. Mark would stay there at night, go through the manufacturers' manuals and find companies around the United States that wanted to buy those items. He was making a nice little profit on the side, but the bosses got upset about it, and he almost got fired over it.

Eventually, Mark left and moved to Pittsburgh, Pennsylvania. But before he left us, while the other guys were driving to work in their pickup trucks, Mark was driving a new white T-Bird. He and his wife were living in a nice house.

Then in Pittsburgh, Mark opened his own business. That was several years ago. He eventually started three businesses and had about sixteen men working for him.

Workers With No Vision

Many of the guys I hired at the same time I hired Mark are still working there in that shop. That's what I find so amazing about this story. You need to bear this in mind; I am making a point here about your kids: The world's system is designed to hold them down and keep them down.

As I mentioned before, those guys were being paid two dollars an hour more than they could get on some other job. In addition, they were given a free turkey at Thanksgiving, a free ham at Christmas and a twelve hundred dollar Christmas bonus. Where else could they get such benefits?

All those guys had much in common: they were about nineteen years old; they had a girlfriend who thought her guy had the world by the tail; they were driving a new pickup truck; and they had a hunting dog and a shotgun. As far as they were concerned, life was great.

By getting that twelve hundred dollar Christmas bonus, they should have been saving some of it. But as with human nature, most people don't save any of it. They were so thrilled to get it that they were going out and buying things like color TV sets and VCRs.

Now for the most part, they were good workers, but they had no vision, no discipline, no idea that God wanted something good to happen in their lives. They didn't really work at getting along with people, and they stayed mad at the company half of the time.

That will bring zero promotion, by the way. If you are griping about your employer, don't expect anything good to happen; God won't let it. If you are badmouthing the place you work, don't look for a raise in your check; it isn't coming. God says you are supposed to be a good employee. If you can't handle it, quit and go to work somewhere else. Until then, pray for favor; pray for that boss who may be mistreating you; do the best job you can, or there will be no promotion.

I know about this. I have been on both sides of the fence.

If nothing is coming your way, you aren't going to force yourself into anything by saying, "Bless God, we'll *make* them give us a raise!" You aren't going to make your boss do anything. If he gave you something, it would be some token gesture. It's not Biblical for you to act that way, and it won't work.

After Mark had been gone for a while, he came back for a visit. It seems he had started contracting out his time because he was so good at what he did. He was making more money than he ever had before. When he came into the office to visit, his beeper kept going off, and he was having to make some phone calls. He had also attended a Bible school.

Mark had the same level of education as those other guys, but his dad had planted a vision inside his heart that God had something great for him.

Those other guys are making about a buck more an hour now than they used to make and are still getting that twelve hundred dollar Christmas bonus. The problem is, their new pickup trucks are now beat to a pulp and their hunting dogs have died. Their girlfriends became their wives, and they now have two or three kids; but they are living in little shacks and are just trying to make ends meet.

Proverbs 29:18 says, **Where there is no *vision*, the people perish.**

A Good Work Ethic

Now in training our high-school students, I would tell them: "People are going to be interviewing you for a job, even if it's to work at McDonald's; and I'll tell you what they're looking for right now." Then I would explain how they should look and act during their interview.

You know, more kids at our school are going on for a college education. As Scripture says, the wealth of the wicked is laid up for the just. (Prov. 13:22.)

You may say, "Well, we can't afford to send our kids to college." But you can. Money is everywhere, and the diligent will get it.

Each year, people from the College Board SAT Program would come to our city and hold an informative seminar for administrators and guidance counselors to let us know what changes had been made on the college entrance exams.

One of the representatives made the astounding comment that colleges and industries were no longer looking for *trained* young people, but for *trainable* young people. He told us that knowledge was exploding all over the earth and that there was enough new information going into the Library of Congress each hour to fill up five sets of encyclopedias. He said with technology increasing as it is, even if a person received a degree, eighteen months after he finished school he might be obsolete. We always need to be learning.

The Bible says that the hand of the diligent (the hardworking one) will bear rule and will be made rich. (Prov. 12:24; 10:4.) So whether our children attend college, receive vocational training, enter the military or start to work on the ground floor of a company, God's will is for them to succeed.

What you purpose, God will help you do. The Holy Spirit will be your Helper. But first you have to put your hand to the plow. You can't just wish you had a plow; you have to find a plow and place your hand on it. Even if you don't like that particular plow, you have to keep plowing with it until you get a better one. Plow well with the one you have and take care of it, because if you are faithful with it, you will get another one.

You have to put into your children the idea that they don't start at the top; they start at the bottom. If they started at the top, it wouldn't last long. If they can get there that quickly, then they can leave there just that quickly. They have to start at the bottom, apply themselves and be a good steward. They have to show up on time and do what they're supposed to do and even above that.

I promise you, if an unbeliever could say of Daniel, "We perceive an excellent spirit in this young man, so let's put him in charge,"[1] then that unbelieving employer you have, who cusses and gripes and fires people, can put you in charge too. As Acts 10:34 says, God is no

---

[1] SEE DANIEL 6:3.

respecter of persons. We just have to do our job. Then as a parent, we have to place that work ethic inside our children.

Always Work *With* God, Not *Without* Him

When we are in church, we hear about how we are to win the world. We are to go out and tell the world how good God is. Do you believe in God? You had better. Are you praying in the Spirit? You had better be. That's how you are going to be led. I wouldn't want to go through life without being filled with the Holy Ghost and letting Him lead me and guide me. But **faith without works is dead** (James 2:26), so we have to do both.

If you are going to work without God, you will work yourself into the grave and be buried early. People may come to your funeral and talk about what a hard worker you were, but you still died early.

I have been there. I have seen this happen to both my family members and my friends. It really hurts, but it's a real eye-opener: We find out that we need to do better than that.

When I stand before God with my children, I want Him to look at all six of them and say to each: "Well done, thou good and faithful servant." I want Him to say that to them, not because they're perfect, but because they kept getting back up every time they had fallen. It goes back to our being righteous.

I want my kids to know what God is saying to them, so I say to them:

"Look, just because you bit the dust doesn't change God's plan. Things may not look good now, but He still has the plans. I want you to know that you have to obey the authority God places in your life. You can't be kicking authority all the time and get anywhere. You have to understand that you are gifted to succeed at something. All you have to do is find out what it is and then get after it. Start stewarding the little part of it, and it will begin to grow. God will begin to add to it as you are able to handle it."

Then the last thing I tell my kids is, "You had better know how to get along with people."

You can have the greatest vision and be the most self-disciplined or most gifted individual in the world. But if you can't get along with people, nobody will give you the time of day, because they don't want to be around you.

So you have to teach your kids how to get along with people, both their friends and their enemies. They have to walk with wisdom toward everyone.

Pray this prayer for us as God's stewards:

Father, thank You right now for the wisdom of Your Word. It's so good, Lord. We have studied enough truth from it in this book to live a lifetime — if we will just do the things we know to do.

Father, help us and give us strength. If we are weak, You said for us to say we are strong. We declare this for ourselves and our families. We know we have weaknesses, but we are going to say what You say and declare, "We are strong in the Lord and in the power of His might!"

Father, though we have fallen many times, we thank You for the cleansing blood of Jesus Christ. We thank You that we have the ability to come to You boldly and to confess our sins; that You are faithful and just to forgive us and to cleanse us from all unrighteousness.

Though we may bite the dust, we will be known as those "getting-up people." We will get up, dust ourselves off, repent, put our hand back on the plow and set ourselves to do great things for You, Father.

I say now by faith that our children will do great things, Father. We don't see them as they are today; we see what they will become. And we, the parents, will be the biggest cheerleaders in our home.

Father, through our example and by Your Word through Your Spirit, teach our children how to be wise stewards over the things You have placed in their hands. Small though it may appear, teach them not to despise the days of small beginnings but to be faithful over little things. For those who will be faithful over little, You will make ruler over much.

I pray in Jesus' name for every child represented, regardless of where they are today. Teach them to be wise stewards, and according to Your Word they shall become rulers over much.

Father, send good friends across our children's paths to sharpen them like iron. You can bring them, Lord, and I thank You for doing that right now. I pray it in Jesus' name. Amen.

12

Favor With Man = Friendship

Luke 2:52 — And Jesus increased in wisdom and stature, and in favour with God and man.

Thus far in our study, we have looked at the subjects of vision, discipline and stewardship. Now let's consider the fourth part of this verse:

And Jesus increased...in *favour with...man.*

Now regarding this phrase, *favor with man,* immediately you may wonder if you have really read the New Testament. You might wonder, how could Jesus have had favor with man? He faced challenges constantly, having to deal with the Sadducees, the Pharisees and the mobs of people who tried to stone Him or throw Him over the cliff. But Jesus just walked through the midst of them. (John 8:59; 10:31,39; Luke 4:28-30.)

Scripture doesn't say, "Jesus had favor with man and therefore was loved by everybody." He knew how to deal not only with His friends but with His enemies. Sometimes He even got onto His best friends. He raised His voice with them because He loved them and wanted to see them changed. He would admonish them and He would encourage them.

The key word I want to use for *favor with man* is *friendship.*

After discussing friendship in general, I will be talking to you about teaching your children how to pick their friends and how to get into a dating relationship. God is big on people getting together, but there are some guidelines we need to follow. Then we will look into the subject of how to teach your children about sex. It will be good, and I will give you some recommended reading.

Show Yourself Friendly

Proverbs 18:24 — **A man that hath friends must shew himself friendly....**

Friends don't appear out of nowhere. The only way you will ever have friends in this life is by showing yourself friendly. God won't just look down someday, feel sorry for you and send lots of friends your way because you are lonely. If you don't show yourself friendly, you will never have any friends.

One time I was counseling a sweet brother in the Lord who had been in America for about two years after leaving his family in another country. He was crying, and when I asked what his problem was, he said, "I have no friend."

"Where are your friends?" I asked.

"They have all moved away."

As we talked, he kept repeating himself. I don't know what he thought I was going to be able to do, maybe sprinkle some magic dust on him, open the closet door and have somebody to jump out and become his friend.

I kept trying to tell him how to fix the problem. I said: "There are places where people gather together, so if you want friends, you have to go where they are. It takes being around people first before you can have a friend." For a while it was a struggle to teach him how to be friendly.

If you go into a room full of people, the whole bunch of them aren't just going to run up to you and clamor over you. If you want friends, you have to show yourself friendly.

This is the Golden Rule: *Do unto others as you would have them do unto you.* Jesus said it this way:

Matthew 7:12 — **Therefore all things whatsoever ye would that men should do to you, do ye even so to them....**

A Real Friend

There are more Scriptures in the Bible having to do with friends than with hell. Just look up the words in a concordance and count all those references. Hell is important and we all should want to avoid it, but there is more to be said about friendship. Any person, including our children, will become like the people he hangs out with.

David Wilkerson, author of *The Cross and the Switchblade*, wrote another book entitled *Parents on Trial*. In it he shares questions he has asked each of the teens in his Teen Challenge program.[1] Their conversation goes something like this:

"How did you end up in this mess? How did you get involved with things like drugs, vandalism, pornography and prostitution?"

Without exception, they all say, "When we began to hang with the wrong crowd."

When he asks them how they got their first snort of dope, they answer, "A friend gave it to me."

"How did you first get into stealing?"

"A friend took me along."

Let me tell you something, Mom and Dad: No matter how many times your kids go through the doors of a church or how many times you make them memorize Scripture, they will become like those they hang out with.

We don't have many real friends, and neither will our kids. We will have lots of acquaintances but very few friends. We may have one, two, maybe three, in our whole lifetime. A real friend is

---

[1] Taken from *How To Raise Good Kids* by Barbara Cook (Minneapolis: Bethany House, 1978), pp. 142,143.

somebody who would lay down his life for us. We need to teach this truth to our children.

As we learned in a previous chapter, a good friend will sharpen us like iron. Scripture says:

Proverbs 27:17 — **Iron sharpeneth iron; so a man sharpeneth the countenance of his friend.**

Do you know what happens when you strike iron? The sparks will fly. Good friendship will cause some sparks to fly. But that's what keeps it sharp.

A real friend will tell you the truth — how you have bad breath or dandruff, or are getting a little pudgy around the middle. Your friend will tell you the truth because he loves you.

An acquaintance won't necessarily tell you the truth. He may just mush you up and then mess you up!

The Value of Christian Training

In 1874 the state of New York had a terrible problem. Its prisons were overcrowded, and new facilities couldn't be built fast enough. The state officials didn't know what to do. So a man named R. A. Dugdale was hired to do some research. He came back with a fascinating report.[2] (I have no idea about Dugdale's spiritual condition. There is nothing in the history books to give us any indication about that.)

Dugdale did a study of two families and their descendants over some six generations to see how the different lifestyles affected their children.

The first half of his report was about a family named Jukes. Both Max Jukes and his brother married sisters. According to the report, neither of them believed in Christian training. (I have no idea what was meant by "Christian training.")

---

[2] TAKEN FROM *GROWING UP GOD'S WAY* BY JOHN A. STORMER (FLORISSANT, MISSOURI: LIBERTY BELL PRESS, 1984), P. 209.

They had 1,026 descendants. Because of their lifestyles, 300 of them died young and many others suffered poor health. Among the descendants, 140 served an average of thirteen years each in prison, 190 were confirmed public prostitutes and 100 were alcoholics. Over a hundred-year period this family cost the state of New York 1.2 million dollars.

The second half of the report compared the Jukes family with another family named Edwards. Jonathan Edwards, whom you might remember from your history books, was a Christian minister who married a girl "of like belief."

Edwards and his wife had 729 descendants. Of those, 300 were preachers, 65 were college professors, 13 were university presidents, 60 were authors, 3 were congressmen and 1 served as vice-president of the United States. With the exception of a grandson named Aaron Burr, who was hanged, this second family cost the state of New York not one single penny.

The difference in these two families was that one family believed in Christian training while the other just raised up their kids and fed them.

Our Children Are Our Reward

Psalm 127:3 — Lo, children are an heritage of the Lord: and the fruit of the womb is his reward.

Our kids will be our reward. Whether that reward is good or bad will be determined by what we do with them. If we feel called to save this world and preach the Gospel to the lost, then we had better be serious about teaching and training our children to follow after God each day of their lives.

Scripture doesn't say we as parents have to be so somber that we never laugh. I believe in laughter as an expression of the joy of the Lord. (Ps. 126:2.)

Sometimes Christians look like they have been sucking on sour pickles. Instead of giving a testimony of what God has done for them, they are always talking about how bad their life was the day before.

But as the Bible says: "Let the redeemed of the Lord say so. Let the weak say, I am strong, and the poor say, I am rich." (Ps. 107:2; Joel 3:10; Prov. 10:22.)

If you keep hanging around the wrong kind of people, you will be thinking just like they think.

Maybe you have never heard some of the principles being covered in this book, but they are Biblical principles. All across our country secular seminars are being held to teach these principles to businessmen. The unbelievers will pick up on them, start using them and leave many of us at the starting gate.

In this study we will be looking at several Scriptures on friendship. We must pay close attention to them, so that we will turn out like the Edwards family and not the Jukes family.

Again, Proverbs 18:24 says, **A man that hath friends must shew himself friendly....** Our children aren't going to grow up and automatically be friendly. It's a skill they have to be taught. They must be taught certain social skills, such as how to carry on a conversation.

Let me show you one way I have worked at training my kids to talk.

The Elevator Game

When being introduced to some people, I have noticed that, instead of looking in my direction, some people will stare down as if something was just dropped on the ground. How are they ever going to win the world for Jesus if they can't even look another person in the face?

Having traveled around the country, I have stayed in lots of big hotels. I remember how intimidated I once was when riding on an elevator with strangers.

As an example, let's say you get on an elevator at the twenty-eighth floor going down to the hotel lobby. If another person gets on when you do, you both stare up at the floor number as if it's so fascinating to watch it change for those twenty-seven floors.

I determined that I wasn't going to do that anymore. So I learned to play what I call the elevator game. Now it drives my kids nuts to get on an elevator with me. That's when I get tenacious. It even scares some people.

As a young boy I was scared to meet people or to get up in front of a class at school. When you are a scared little boy, you aren't going anywhere. Scared people will never have anything and will never get anywhere. Proverbs 28:1 says, **...the righteous are bold as a *lion*** — not like a little kitty cat.

So now whenever I get on an elevator with a stranger, the first thing I do, even before the door closes, is to start talking. I ask people questions like: "What's your name? What are you doing here — on vacation? Have you ever been here before? What is there to see around this area?"

I don't always know what to say; I just open my mouth and start talking.

I would practice the elevator game with the kids at school and with my kids at home on Saturday morning. My kids didn't really like playing that game, so they would always say, "Oh, Dad, not this morning — please." But that didn't stop me.

Selecting one of them to be the contestant, I said, "Come on...stand up." I looked at my watch and said, "You have five minutes to talk, and there's a penalty if you don't go that long." Then I gave them a subject to talk about. The moment I said, "Go," they had to start talking to me and just keep talking until I told them to stop.

As an example, let's say I picked tennis shoes as the subject. When I said, "Go," that kid would begin talking, sounding something like this:

"I like tennis shoes. I have a pair; in fact, I have several pairs. Tennis shoes are made in several different colors. Some of mine are worn out. I don't have any shoestrings in them right now, but I'm going to get some shoestrings. I use my tennis shoes to run and to play basketball. Sometimes I don't know where they are, and I'll have to look for them. Sometimes my mom yells at me because I don't know where they are. I even lost a pair of them one time. They sure cost a lot of money — $85.95 a pair!"

Now do you get the idea? You might want to try it with your kids.

Teach Your Kids To Be Friendly

Strongly encourage your kids to speak up, to look people in the eye, to shake hands with them. Most businessmen say that they can tell how a business deal will go with a person by the way that person shakes hands.

Kids have to learn how to be friendly. It's a skill, but they can learn it. Anybody can learn it.

But if our kids don't ever learn to be friendly, they will be susceptible to the first person who shows any sign of affection toward them. Somebody will be trying to draw from our kids, but I don't want anybody except me drawing anything out of my children. That's my job as a parent.

Make Sure Your Friend

Proverbs 27:10 says, **Thine own friend, and thy father's friend, forsake not....** Just because you had a friend once doesn't mean that person will stay your friend forever. You have to make sure that friend.

Friends don't just automatically stay friends. They don't become card-carrying members of the Friendship Club and say, "You're my friend forever, even if I never talk to you again." That isn't how it works.

If you intend to keep a friend, you have to do as the Bible says: continually show yourself friendly and make sure your friend.

Think about it: Have you sent your friend a card lately or given your friend a call or taken your friend out to eat? Why don't you run over to your friend's house and see if you can be of help with anything? There will come a day when you will have need of a friend, maybe even a lot of friends. It's always good to have friends.

A Friend Can Be Your Closest Companion

Proverbs 17:17 — **A friend loveth at all times, and a brother is born for adversity.**

Sometimes your closest companion won't be somebody of your own blood, but a friend. That's hard for some people, especially Southerners, to believe, but it's the truth.

Let's look again at Proverbs 27:17, which says, **Iron sharpeneth iron; so a man sharpeneth the countenance of his friend.** A good friend will sharpen you and make you a better person.

As mentioned earlier in this chapter, when iron sharpens iron, sparks fly. That means true friends will be honest with you and will always tell you the truth. If you just want people to lie to you, you don't need a real friend; you just need to be surrounded by a bunch of people.

The Bible teaches us to mark those given to flattery. As Scripture says:

Proverbs 29:5,6 TLB[3] — **Flattery is a trap; evil men are caught in it, but good men stay away and sing for joy.**

Proverbs 20:19 — **He that goeth about as a talebearer revealeth secrets: therefore meddle not with him that flattereth with his lips.**

You need to teach your kids about flattery. They are most susceptible to it when they aren't receiving any praise at home. The degree to which somebody flatters you to your face is the degree to which they can plunge a knife into your back. So teach your kids to watch out for flattery. Flattery is just a lot of cheap words.

Friendship is so important, and I want my children to have good friends. One of the most important things I pray every day for my kids is that they will find good friends. My prayer goes something like this:

Father, I thank You for giving my children godly friends, those who will sharpen them like iron. Send my children some good friends who will sharpen them and keep them sharp. If You have to, move those good friends in from another state. I pray that if any of their friends won't sharpen them You will just move them out of the way.

This sounds strong until you see the results of poor friendships. Your child's poor selection of friends can be devastating.

This is a good prayer for you to pray too. Just thank God every day that your kids will have good friends.

We Cannot Survive Alone

Ecclesiastes 4:9,10 says:

Two are better than one; because they have a good reward for their labour.

---

[3] *THE LIVING BIBLE* (WHEATON, ILLINOIS: TYNDALE, 1971).

For if they fall, the one will lift up his fellow: but woe to him that is alone when he falleth; for he hath not another to help him up.

Verse 12 says:

...and a threefold cord is not quickly broken.

In other words, this means the more the better; we cannot survive alone.

That's why the Bible says:

Hebrews 10:24,25 — **Let us consider one another to provoke unto love and to good works:**

Not forsaking the assembling of ourselves together, **as the manner of some is; but exhorting one another: and so much the more, as ye see the day approaching.**

There will be times when you are to be a blessing to others and they are to be a blessing to you. It's a mutual benefit set up by God.

As believers, we are not to forsake the assembling of ourselves together in these last days. God's people need one another. We need more than ever to be involved somewhere in church — in a youth group, in children's church, in an adult Bible study. We need to be with fellow believers. We are commanded to come together in the name of the Lord. We need one another; we cannot survive alone.

Don't get out there by yourself and be isolated. You must realize that there are no perfect people, no perfect families, no perfect kids. But there are strong people, strong families and strong kids. Not perfect but strong through God.

As a church, we have leaned on the world too long. God has given us the light and the glory, but we have been going to the darkness and the dead to find out what to do about our problems. The darkness and the dead won't help us. We have to leave there and go back to what God has said in His Word.

Righteous people bite the dust on a regular basis. What are you to do when you fall to the ground? Get up, spit out the rocks and dirt from your mouth, dust yourself off, repent to God, put your hand back on the plow and start moving again.

Now remember, every chance he gets, the devil will come at you with guilt. He will make you feel bad about what you have done or failed to do as a parent. He will make you think that life is just made for hanging on and surviving. But God is saying you can thrive.

Don't Be the Friend of an Angry Man

Proverbs 22:24,25 says:

Make no friendship with an angry man; and with a furious man thou shalt not go:

Lest thou learn his ways, and get a snare to thy soul.

If you hang around someone who is always losing his temper, you will begin to think that is how you should act. You will think that by losing your temper you will get what you want. How you react to situations will label you.

I don't want to learn the ways of an angry person. I don't want to be around anyone who can't control himself. If you can't control yourself, you will end up hurting somebody. I would swing a wide path around someone like that.

Be Careful When Picking Close Friends

As Scripture says, "Don't be deceived, for evil associations will corrupt good manners." (See 1 Cor. 15:33 AMP.) You can have a good child who has good morals and has been taught good manners, but evil associations will corrupt him. Proverbs 14:7 says:

Go from the presence of a foolish man, when thou perceivest not in him the lips of knowledge.

How do you tell your children who to stay away from and who to get close to?

We are commanded by God to love every single person on this planet. There is no option. As I tell my kids: "You are commanded in the Word of God to love everybody — whatever the situation. If somebody is thirsty, give him some water. If he's hungry, feed him. If he's in the hospital or prison, go visit him. If his car is stuck in a ditch, help pull him out. If he's moving away, help load the truck."

But when it comes to friendships — the people we spend our spare time with — God is very specific. Doing things for other people doesn't mean we are obligated to sit down and have lunch with them. We are not required to spend our spare time with them. We have to teach our kids this truth.

There are some twenty-two traits given in the Bible, as in 2 Timothy 3:1-5, that we really ought to watch out for in people. Let's look at this passage:

2 Timothy 3:1-5 — **This know also, that in the last days perilous times shall come.**

For men shall be lovers of their own selves, covetous, boasters, proud, blasphemers, disobedient to parents, unthankful (which is why we need to teach our kids to say thank you), **unholy,**

Without natural affection, trucebreakers, false accusers, incontinent, fierce, despisers of those that are good (which covers the media making fun of God's people),

Traitors, heady, highminded, lovers of pleasures more than lovers of God;

Having a form of godliness, but denying the power thereof: from such turn away.

This Scripture is telling us to get away from people like this. We don't have to hang around them.

You might say, "But I thought Christians are to love everybody."

Yes, that's what the Bible says. But that doesn't mean we have to sit down and eat lunch with everybody. If you are hungry, I will feed you, but I am not just automatically going to spend my spare time with you.

Kids Should Be Cautious Around Strangers

Sometimes children are taught to be friendly to everybody. But I don't want my children to be friendly to just anybody, and I have taught them that. There are some people my kids should avoid being around.

I remember one time when an old friend was visiting in town. He was a real hugging, back-patting kind of guy. But when he reached over to hug Corrie, my middle daughter, she politely but firmly said, "Please don't touch me." He was a good guy, but kids don't always know that.

My kids have been taught how certain people may try to take advantage. We have heard about child abductions — how some stranger, being really friendly, will come up to a kid and ask for directions. I have warned my kids to watch out for this. So they don't have any fear about it; they just have knowledge.

As God's Word says, **My people are destroyed for lack of knowledge** (Hos. 4:6). We can be friendly when we know the boundaries. Instead of hiding in a hole and being scared about everything, we can have knowledge of the Word. **So then faith cometh by hearing, and hearing by the word of God** (Rom. 10:17). We are to do everything we know to do; then God will do the rest. He is faithful.

Disrespect of Parents

Again, one of the traits mentioned in 2 Timothy 3, is disobedience to parents.

We are very careful not to let kids come into our house and start talking trash about their mom and dad. When they do this, we quickly correct them. If they continue to dishonor their parents, that's the last time they will be invited to our home. I don't want my kids around those who are running down their parents.

Ephesians 6:2,3 says, **Honour thy father and mother...That it may be well with thee, and thou mayest live long on the earth.** When kids are showing dishonor toward their mom and dad, they will pay a price for it in this life. I don't want my child learning their ways.

Listening to Bad Talk From Other Kids at School

We also have to teach our children how to handle certain traits in other people. Our kids can be caught in some compromising situations.

They might be hanging around other kids in the hall at school when all of a sudden those kids start talking trash. If our kids don't back away immediately, they may find themselves laughing along with the rest of them at something they shouldn't be laughing at and sounding like a bunch of hyenas.

Our kids can see if the conversation isn't going anywhere. They don't have to make a big religious scene out of it. They don't have to stay there and condemn the others by preaching to them. They just need to ease on down the hall, saying, "Well, it's time to go; I have to get to class."

Proverbs 14:7 says, **Go from the presence of a foolish man, when thou perceivest not in him the lips of knowledge.**

With some wisdom, our children can avoid embarrassing situations. So we need to teach our children how to back out of those situations and not get caught up in them.

Finally, a life-changing experience would be for a family to get a concordance and a Bible, to look up about 103 Scripture verses on the subject of friends and friendship and to write them out longhand. You and your family will never be the same. You can't have a friend until you know how to be one.

Let's look next into the subject of dating. Now that we know how to choose our friends, it will help the process of choosing a lifetime mate. After all, our spouse is our best friend.

13

This Dating Thing

Now having dealt with friendship, let's go on to this dating thing. The whole idea behind friendship is that our kids will eventually get into dating.

Every person yearns for love, and most look for it in marriage. More than ninety percent of all the people in the United States will marry at least once in their lifetime. But each year in the United States, more than two hundred thousand marriages end prior to the couple's second anniversary, mostly because they decided too quickly, were too young and had unrealistic expectations.

The number of unmarried teenagers getting pregnant has nearly doubled in the past two decades. Though rare in the early 1960s, by the late 1980s nearly one in ten unmarried teenage girls got pregnant. According to the American Enterprise Institute, teenage sexual activity will result in nearly one million pregnancies annually.[1] That's bad!

By age twenty, 81 percent of today's unmarried males and 67 percent of today's unmarried females have had sexual intercourse.[2] Now this doesn't sound very good. What's the problem?

Most of the young people we have counseled in this area are born-again, Spirit-filled, church-going Christians. So there must be something wrong. Why are they having to deal with these problems?

[1] WILLIAM J. BENNETT, THE INDEX OF LEADING CULTURAL INDICATORS, VOL. 1 (MARCH 1993), P. 8.

[2] JOSH MCDOWELL AND DICK DAY, WHY WAIT (SAN BERNARDINO, CALIFORNIA: HERE'S LIFE PUBLISHERS, 1987), P. 21.

Kids Don't Relate to Their Parent's Past

Listen to this carefully, Mom and Dad: God's Word doesn't say He will watch over *your* testimony to perform it; it says He will watch over *His* Word to perform it. (Jer. 1:12 AMP.) We really don't have any business telling our children about what we did or didn't do as a young person. Once we have repented, it's nobody's business what we repented of. According to Scripture, the moment we repented, God took our transgressions as far as the east is from the west and cast them into the depths of the sea. (Ps. 103:12; Mic. 7:19.)

Now, as mentioned earlier, I married my childhood sweetheart. Denise is the first girl I dated and the first girl I kissed. A year and a half later, we were married. But not everyone is that way.

I can't just say to my kids, "You're going to be like your mother and me." God may have a different set of steps for them.

So you don't have to share everything about your past life with your kids, thinking it will help them in some way. As Scripture says, God watches over *His* Word to perform it — not our life story. I do believe in sharing the great things God has done, passing on the faith to the next generation. But my former life as a sinner gives no glory to God; neither does it build faith in my children. So, instead, let's tell them what the Word says.

Kids Who Think They Are in Love

One day while in the middle of a class at school, I noticed two high school students sitting there. I could see they were "in love." Having swapped rings, they had that lovesick look about them. She was wearing his ring on her finger with lots of masking tape wrapped around it, and he wore hers on a little chain around his neck. During the chapel service, they were sitting close to one another, closer than they were supposed to.

I shouldn't have done this, but I called them out and said, "I want the two of you to stand up for a minute. You must really be in love. This is getting serious, isn't it?"

The guy just stood there like a tree stump. I said a few more things, then finally the girl fired back at me, "That's right, Mr. McGee. We're planning to get married."

When she said that, his eyes widened just a bit. I could see that his buddies were snickering and making comments among themselves. His ship was slowly sinking. Obviously, he hadn't seen the relationship progressing quite as far as she had.

Then I said: "I'm really impressed that you two young people can make such a mature decision at such a young age. That's difficult for a lot of young people to do. I know you love God and His Word. The Bible has so many Scriptures on friendship, and I know you've based your relationship on the Word of God. Would you please tell me one of those Scriptures on friendship that your relationship is based on?"

Again, the guy just stared at me. He wasn't really listening; he just looked scared.

Finally, the girl thought up a Scripture and spoke out in a questioning tone, "A friend sticketh closer than a brother?"

"Okay, you can sit down," I said.

It seems too often these days that young people think they are in love when they can't even spell the word!

The typical thing is for the guy to drive up in front of his girl's house in his souped-up car or his daddy's clunker (whichever he can get) and blow the horn, and the girl starts toward the door.

"Where are you going?" her daddy asks.

"Out," she says.

"Really? Where?"

"Oh, just out," she responds.

Wrong answer!

If she were my daughter and she said that to me, I would just respond by saying, "If you don't know where you're going, you might get lost, so you can just stay right here."

An Assignment to My Students

As I mentioned earlier, every year I taught a course to our seniors on developing a Biblical world view. At the beginning of the year I had them select a subject to investigate. So they chose subjects like crime, the economy, abortion, sports and money. Then I said:

"Now for the next month I want you to look through the newspaper every day, find an article on that subject, cut it out and put it in a scrapbook. At the end of the quarter you're to write a one-page summary paper, based on those forty-five articles, telling what has been going on with that subject and what the world says about it.

"Next, I want you to take your concordance and your Bible, look up twenty-five Scriptures about your subject and find out what God has to say about it. Then you are to get up in front of the class and in five minutes tell us the difference between those two views based on your research.

"I don't care what subject you may pick. Whatever the world has been saying about that subject for the past nine weeks, God has been saying exactly the opposite for the last two thousand years.

"Newspapers don't necessarily contain the whole truth. It isn't that the newspapermen show up at work and talk about how they can lie to the public that day. But most of them have no knowledge of God. They are ever learning but never able to come to the knowledge of the truth."

I would show my students how God thinks the opposite of whatever the world is saying. He is at enmity with the world, being at opposite ends of the scale from the world.

Along with that scrapbook, they kept a second scrapbook which included information from the newspaper on births, deaths, marriages, divorces and people caught driving drunk. For the first week, all they did was find the names people gave to their new babies. It was kind of cute for those first few days.

Then the second week I said: "Now we're going to do something different. I want you to look down through the list of new births from all the hospitals and see how many moms are listed as giving birth to a baby without the daddy's name being given, implying a single mother who has given birth."

In that nine-month period, we found that in our city thirty-three percent of the time the daddy's name was never listed next to the mother's.

Then I said: "Now, let's pick out one of these mothers. Here's a girl named Jennifer. It says she had a little baby girl yesterday, but the daddy's name isn't mentioned here in the paper. Where do suppose he is this morning?"

Those kids just looked at me.

I said: "Think about it. He's probably at home with his own mother this morning eating Cheerios, while she does his laundry and everything else for him. Then later on today, he'll probably hang around with the guys and play some Nintendo. But Jennifer won't be going out and doing any of those fun things; she has a newborn baby to take care of."

After nine months of cutting out this information from the newspapers, several girls told me how they felt about it. One said: "Mr. McGee, when I was out on a date the other night, that guy was really giving me the line. But, you know, all I could see was that section of the newspaper showing how those mothers gave birth to little babies with no support from the daddies."

The Story of Two Bald Eagles

I want to give you a story that I always tell teenagers when I talk on dating and courtship. This story is about bald eagles and how they mate. There are lots of bald eagles in our part of the state of Oklahoma, down on the river.

The bald eagle has a unique mating ritual. Now to appreciate the story, you have to understand that female bald eagles are always bigger than males. That's just a fact of nature.

In the story I tell, there are two eagles, a female and a male. To add a personal touch, I will give them names: Ernestine is the female and Ernie is the male.

Ernestine gets up one morning and, like eagles do every morning, she goes out flying, looking for some food. Then Ernie sees her flying up high, so he comes up right behind her and says, "Wow, Ernestine, you're looking good today!" She looks around, sees him looking at her and realizes that he is making a move for her.

She flies down to the river bank and picks up a little stick. Then she takes it back up about eight or ten thousand feet and begins a figure-eight movement in the air. She works at building up speed, and when she hits maximum speed, she lets go of that stick.

Being the gentleman that he is, Ernie dives for the stick, grabs it and brings it back to her. But Ernestine won't take it.

She flies back down to the river bank, gets a bigger stick, carries it up about six or eight thousand feet and starts the figure-eight again, building up speed.

Ernie is behind her again, yelling out, "Ernestine, you're looking good!"

When Ernestine hits maximum speed, she lets go of the stick. Again being the gentleman, Ernie dives for it, grabs it and brings it back to her. But again she refuses it.

Ernestine repeats this process over and over. It's said that a mature female bald eagle can pick up the equivalent of an eight-foot fence post.

Again, Ernestine flies down to the river bank, this time picking up a small log and stirring the dust as she gets it off the ground. She takes it up about five hundred feet, starts the figure-eight and builds up speed.

Ernie, flying right behind her, is thinking, *What a female I have found!*

But this time, when Ernestine lets go of that log and Ernie takes off after it, he doesn't realize that he is now past the point of no return. Male eagles have been known to die trying to catch that log. Some of them snap their wings trying to stop it, others fly straight into the water, while still others hit the ground with a thud.

If Ernie, realizing he can't stop the log before it hits the ground, chickens out and lets go of it, then Ernestine will dive down, attack him and either run him off or kill him in a fight.

If Ernie had been able to stop that log and hold it there, even momentarily, Ernestine would then have mated with him for life. Here's why: Come late winter or early spring when she is sitting in the nest on top of those eggs and, early one cold morning, the snow is hitting her in the face, she wants to know beforehand, not afterward, that Ernie will be capable of bringing home the "bacon" that morning.

"Too Close Too Soon"

Sexual intercourse does not just happen; it is a result of choices that are made. There are several steps leading up to sexual intercourse, step one usually being that of holding hands, followed by a series of other steps.

In their book *Too Close Too Soon*, Jim Talley and Bobbie Reed estimate that it takes a boy and a girl about three hundred hours of spending time alone together before their relationship develops from casual acquaintance to a sexually active involvement. That means if they go out on a date every Friday and Saturday night for four-to-five hours each night, it will take them about seven months to reach that point. TOO CLOSE TOO SOON![3]

One day in November several years ago a young couple came to my office at school, knocked on my door and said, "Mr. McGee, can we see you?"

Both of them were seniors, and they planned to be married the following June. They were born again and Spirit-filled, as were their parents, and everybody seemed to be in agreement about the marriage.

"Come on in," I said. "Have a seat."

They sat down and then just stared at me. He took a deep breath, and then tears came into her eyes.

"Is there a problem?" I asked.

"Yes, Mr. McGee, we need some help."

They just sat there and stared at me some more. Then it dawned on me what the problem might be.

"Have you two committed fornication?" I asked.

The young man's eyes opened wide, and he drew a deep breath. Then he said, "No, sir, we haven't."

But she added, "We've come awfully close though." Then she began to cry and said, "We're concerned and scared. We think we're seeing too much of one another."

"Well, what do you want me to do?" I asked.

---

[3] (NASHVILLE: THOMAS NELSON, 1982), PP. 33,41.

"We don't know, Mr. McGee. We think maybe we need to break up for about three months and just not see one other. What do you think?"

"I think that's probably a good idea."

It's amazing what kids will do sometimes when they have heard the Word of God. They will do what they have heard. They came to me for some advice and some wisdom, so I said: "I'll tell you what we'll do: I'll call your parents and have them come down here. Then I want you to repeat to them what you just told me. I can promise you, they'll help you stay apart for the next three months."

And they did stay apart. Then when June came, they didn't get married; instead, they were married in August of that year.

Today they are the parents of some beautiful children, and both of them are working in the church. I still see them from time to time, and I think, *Great couple! Great marriage!* But there is a unique twist to this story: They didn't marry each other! They came very close, but they each married someone else that August!

I have had kids to sit in my office and say, "I just did it once, Mr. McGee. Honest to God, just once!"

I would say, "I understand; but if you sow human seed, you will reap human crop." That's just a natural, biological law.

The world today is trying to do something with the problems of sexual promiscuity and the abundance of babies being born to young people. But they want to fix it by working on steps eleven and twelve. Unfortunately, it can't be done that way. We have to go back to the beginning and start working at step number one.

God Warns Against Sin

In Jeremiah 29, there are some principles we will look at which I think can be used to relate to dating and its pattern.

If you read back in Scripture, you will see that the prophet Jeremiah knew the people of Israel would be going away for seventy years. They had been sinning, and God had warned them many times through the prophet, saying, "If you don't repent, judgment is coming." But they refused to repent.

So God spoke through Jeremiah to a group of teenage boys who were being carried away captive out of Jerusalem to Babylon. In effect, He was saying to them: "Gentlemen, you're going on a little trip, and you won't be back for seventy years. But I'll tell you how you can handle your life over the next seventy years and prosper."

God is merciful, longsuffering and very forgiving. He will warn His people forever and a day before something happens.

God's Warning to Nineveh

That's exactly what we can see in the book of Jonah. God told Jonah to go and warn the people of Nineveh that they needed to quit sinning. (Jonah 1:2.) But Jonah didn't want to go. He was probably thinking, *If I go over there, those wicked people are going to repent,* and he didn't want them to repent.

Those people had done some really bad things, but God didn't want to kill them; He wanted them to stop sinning. All God ever wants people to do is to stop sinning.

Jonah went in a direction that was different from God's instruction and, as a result, was taken in the belly of a whale and dumped onto the shore. Again, God told him to go to Nineveh and preach His message. (Jonah 3:1.) Finally, Jonah got there. I think he probably gave some wimpy little sermon, telling the people, "You had better quit all of that sin!"

The Bible tells how all of the people — from the king down to the least of the nation — repented in sackcloth and ashes. (Jonah 3:5-10.) God didn't send judgment on them for another four hundred years. Is that long-suffering, or what? All God ever wants is for people to stop sinning and to repent.

The Man of God Speaks

Then one day, as mentioned in the book of Jeremiah, King Nebuchadnezzar and the Babylonians in all their fury came against Israel. They were killing, pillaging and burning. Things were bad. When the day was over, not many people were left and Jerusalem was on fire.

When this occurred, a group of teenage boys, thought to be the smartest, best-looking and most prominent in the community, were gathered up and taken hostage. Among them were Daniel, Shadrach, Meshach and Abednego. (See Dan. 1:1-7.)

It could have happened like this: These boys are being led out of Jerusalem on a dirt road. Their hands are tied, and Babylonian soldiers are on either side of them. Then they look back at the city and realize they won't be eating supper at their mama's table that night.

Then down the road comes the prophet Jeremiah.

Now in those days nobody liked the prophets and they didn't get invited to supper. Prophets were seen as having three bad traits: they ate weird food, dressed in weird clothes and always told the truth.

When those teenage boys looked up and saw that prophet coming, they must have thought: *Thank God, finally the old man is here! Surely he will call thirty she-bears out of the caves to kill all these heathens, or send lightning down from the sky and burn their scalps to a frazzle, or open the ground and swallow up their chariots!*

They were waiting for the man of God to speak, and here's what he said:

Jeremiah 29:4,5 — **Thus saith the Lord of hosts, the God of Israel, unto all that are carried away captives, whom I have caused to be carried away from Jerusalem unto Babylon;**

Build ye houses....

About this time Shadrach probably looked over at Daniel and said, "What did that old man say?"

Daniel said, "I think he said something about building a house."

They probably were thinking, *He must have eaten too many wild locusts — his brain is gone!*

Seven Points to Dating

Let's read on in this passage of Scripture. Then I will break it down and comment as we go.

Jeremiah 29:5-7 — **Build ye houses, and dwell in them; and plant gardens, and eat the fruit of them;**

Take ye wives, and beget sons and daughters; and take wives for your sons, and give your daughters to husbands, that they may bear sons and daughters; that ye may be increased there, and not diminished.

And seek the peace of the city whither I have caused you to be carried away captives, and pray unto the Lord for it: for in the peace thereof shall ye have peace.

I see in this passage of Scripture a list of seven points to dating. In paraphrasing, here's what the prophet was saying:

Step Number One: *Build a house.* In other words, get yourself a place to live; you won't be living with your mama.

Step Number Two: *Dwell in it.* In other words, set up housekeeping. You need things like furniture to sit on and to eat off of; eating utensils like plates, cups, knives, forks and spoons; and everyday household items like toilet paper, toothpaste and light bulbs.

Step Number Three: *Plant a garden.* Paraphrasing from the agricultural society, to me that's saying, *Get a job!* In order for you to have a place to live and a house to keep up, you must get a job.

Step Number Four: *Eat the fruit of it.* Can you eat what you are growing? In other words, can you keep that job? Will it sustain you? Is it working for you?

Once you have those basics — a place in which to live, a house to keep up and a job that will pay your living expenses — then you can go on to the next step.

Step Number Five: *Take a wife (or husband).* In other words, find yourself a girlfriend (or boyfriend) and then get married.

Step Number Six: *Now you can have a baby.* These days too many people jump straight to step six. We will be looking into this aspect of life in further detail, but first let's complete the list with step seven.

Step Number Seven: *Pray for God's peace in your life and live by it.* Follow these first six steps as God's direction for your life; then you can know and live in His peace.

Now back to Step Six.

Guys Can Really Spout a Line

A guy can be out there spouting a line to the gal while his mama is still doing everything for him at home, including washing his underwear.

You see, God created women to be helpmeets for men, so that as heirs together they can fulfill God's plan for their lives as a couple. But if a guy isn't going anywhere, a woman can't be any help to him.

The way I see it, God created my daughters to be helpmeets for young men who are going somewhere. When a young man isn't going anywhere, he has no vision for his life. So that means he has no need of my daughter. He doesn't need help going nowhere; he can do that just fine all by himself.

A guy can really spout a line to a girl, saying things like: "I just love you, baby. You're the only one for me. I'll follow you all the days of my life. There will never be anyone for me but you." But words are cheap.

As stated earlier, young people become too close too soon. They don't need to spend too much time together when they have nothing to do. They can be the ugliest man and the ugliest woman in the world, but if they are put together long enough, something biological will probably happen.

I will give you some illustrations here, then go further into dating.

Functions of the Physical Body

Thanksgiving is a wonderful time of the year. Let's say you wake up one Thanksgiving morning and are lying there in bed. Without even opening your eyes, you can tell what day it is. All you have to do is take a whiff of the air. You can smell all the turkey, ham, sweet-potato casserole and apple pie being prepared in the kitchen.

Just by smelling, your mouth starts to release some saliva. Then your stomach releases those amino acids. You haven't as yet seen or tasted any food, but your body is ready for it. You didn't have to intercede for three days or confess it or ask God for your body to get ready to eat; it just happened. That's a God-given function of your physical body.

Using another example, let's say one night you have been helping out at church as a blessing to your pastor. There happened to be a storm that night and, as a result, the electricity is off. Now everybody has gone home, and you are the last person to leave the building. You walk across the parking lot and all the lights are out, so it's dark and the wind is blowing.

While trying to unlock your car door, you have to bend down to see in the dark. Suddenly, someone jumps out from behind the car and cries, "Boo!" At that moment your body releases a shot of adrenalin into your system. You don't have to pray and ask God for it. That's a God-given function of the physical body.

God is so good to give us options, and you have two: either fight or run. You have the energy to do either. God leaves that choice up to you. So you size it up quickly, and function accordingly.

A third example would be a boy and girl who are sitting in a car. They might just be holding hands or they might be passionately kissing. At some point in their relationship, their physical anatomies will release a shot of blood to their sexual organs in anticipation of sexual intercourse. They don't need to jump up and rebuke the devil; he isn't responsible. This is a God-given bodily function.

According to Proverbs 6:27, when there is fire in a man's bosom, even his clothes will be burned. No man can put it out.

These young people have passed a point that they never should have reached to begin with. Maybe they had already been told, "Now always remember, don't do anything to hurt your daddy." But that won't hold water. When they find themselves together like this in the car, it's as if Dad and Mom have moved off to some other planet.

How To Establish a Standard for Courtship

As parents, we will never be able to really hold our children with our own words. The only things that will hold them are God's Word put inside them and the Holy Spirit working together with that Word.

Now, Mom and Dad, let's look at some pointers on how to establish a standard for courtship. My words are not intended as "Thus saith the Lord" but "Thus saith Joe McGee." These are based upon my study of God's Word, my years of counseling parents and young people and my experiences as a school administrator and children's minister.

I can share my own experiences and the standards I have set for my kids that I feel have worked for a lot of other families. But don't use these standards as your own; they won't necessarily work for you. You need to set up your own system using your own standards, based on your convictions of what the Bible says.

Unless you set a standard for your kids, they will have no idea where the boundary line is drawn, so create your own standard for them. They will either love you for it or eventually hate you because you didn't make them do right.

On more than one occasion in counseling sessions, I have seen young people sit there and scream at their parents for not making them do right. Those are the same kids who at one time were screaming for their parents to give them more freedom. Kids want somebody to tell them what to do. They are saying, "Please show me the right way." But a parent can't be a dictator over them.

According to research that was done by two professors — one from Utah State University and another from Brigham Young University — among twenty-four hundred teens, the younger a girl begins to date, the more likely she is to have sex before graduating from high school. Of girls who began dating at age twelve, 91 percent had sex before graduation, compared to 20 percent who began dating at age sixteen.[4] That isn't even "Thus saith the Lord"; it's just a natural statistic.

But remember this: there is no condemnation and there should be no guilt. That's why we have the blood of Jesus. Nobody is perfect; everybody has sinned — mom, dad and young person. We aren't talking about the past but about the future — our next generation. We, the parents, must pass the wisdom of God on to our children. God has a better way of doing things — better than the world has taught us.

Set an Age To Begin Dating

Our family standard for dating is a series of steps.

---

[4] McDowell and Day, *Why Wait*, p. 79.

Step number one: No child will be allowed to date before age sixteen.

Again, you need to make up your own set of standards. Take this example of my standard and use it as you choose: throw out parts of it, slice it, dice it, maybe use a part of it.

Step number two: When some guy asks one of my daughters for a date, her answer is always the same: "My dad has my social calendar and all my dates are screened through him. I'll be glad to go out with you; you just have to call Dad."

If some guy she doesn't want to date asks her out, she has time to get to me. She doesn't have to lie, telling him, "Oh, I have lots to do tonight, so I can't possibly go out with you."

On the other hand, if the guy is someone she is interested in, she can run home quickly and say, "Daddy, this neat guy is going to call, and I really want to go out with him. Can you do something quick?"

One thing this does is take the heat off my daughters from guys putting pressure on them.

Now by requiring them to talk with me first, I have eliminated every wimp who would even think about spending time alone with my daughter. If that young man doesn't have enough hair on his lip to face a big teddy bear like me, he certainly doesn't deserve to spend one-on-one time with my daughter. I have no qualms about that at all. What would he do when out on a date with my daughter if somebody attacked him? Would he turn around and run, leaving my daughter just standing there?

The "First Date" Is With Dad

Step number three: The "first date" is to be between the young man and me (or her mother).

Once the young man agrees to call and ask for a date with my daughter, he finds that his "first date" is with me. He is required to face me before he will be allowed to date my daughter. I invite him to come over to the house and spend some time with me, or perhaps I can meet him someplace.

I don't mean he can just come by thirty minutes early and visit with me before taking my daughter out on their first date. I intend for him to spend time alone with me. We might eat some pie and drink some coffee, or shoot some basketball, or maybe even go to a ball game.

I want to get to know that young fellow before I will allow him to go anywhere with my girl.

The main question I always ask the guy is: "What do you see yourself doing five years from now?" I ask this same question to every boy who wants to date a daughter of mine. I want to know if he is thinking about the future. The purpose of dating is to find a mate. If my daughter's role is to be a helpmeet, she needs to know what she would be helping him to do.

I want these boys to be real. I don't want them just spouting out something that they have memorized; I want them to think seriously about what they might do with their lives.

Five Dates With the Family

Step number four: The next four or five dates will be with the whole family.

If the young man makes it past the point of that first date with me, I will permit him to start dating my girl. But the next four or five dates are to be with us as a family. (That doesn't include going to church, by the way. I can't really get to know a person when we are sitting in a church pew.)

These first few dates as a family might include doing things together like going to ball games. These times allow me to see this guy act and react. I want him to unlock his jaw and let me hear him talk, because out of the abundance of the heart the mouth will speak.

The Double Date

Step number five: After those four or five dates with the family, then double dates are allowed.

The double date is with a preapproved agenda, which is to be brought to me in writing, and is with another couple, which again I have approved. Let me give you an example.

Suppose the young man tells me they will be at Mazzio's Pizza at 9:15. That means if I pick up the phone at 9:17, call Mazzio's and ask to speak to my daughter, she had better come to the phone.

I expect my daughter to be home by 11:00 p.m., and I expect her date to be at his home by 11:30. In fact, I would call his house to make sure he got there.

"Did your son make it home okay?" I ask.

"Oh, yes, he's here," they say. "Thanks, Mr. McGee; we appreciate your calling."

"No problem," I say. "Goodnight."

I don't want that young man to be out running around late at night; he needs to be home. That's why God made the sun go down. After the sun has set, people should be settling in.

A Single Date

Here's the kicker:

Step number six: Single dates are allowed only after high-school graduation.

My daughters are allowed to go on a single date with a guy as soon as they get their high-school diplomas. That's after he has had his first date with me and I am given a preapproved agenda, showing where he is taking her on their double dates.

Do you know what happens when they go out on that single date? That young man may be looking into my daughter's beautiful eyes, but whose face will he see? *Mine!* I will be there in spirit and in truth! He can't go anywhere without me!

If you will do this, Mom and Dad, you will elevate the value of your daughter in every boy's eyes.

My Daughters Aren't Wallflowers

Some people may say, "I bet your daughters have no social life." But the opposite is true.

My kids are among the most socially active in their schools, and my daughters are the most beautiful you could ever lay your eyes on. Thank God, they look like their mother!

We owned a 1986 Ford Aerostar Van which we had bought brand new, and in five years we had put 234,000 miles on it. In December of the following year we bought a Suburban, and in only one year it had 54,000 miles on it. I would call that being more than "socially active." The way we see it: our children are worth it.

"Pay Now, or Pay Later"

That's why when we talk to our children, they listen. It's not because we are being like dictators; we are just creating a relationship with them. We know them and we are there for them.

As a parent, you either pay now or you will pay later. You may think you don't have time, but you are going to pay with time. I would much rather pay it now. You have to set up a situation with your kids where they know you and trust you, and you know them.

We are not dictators who are always following our children around. But we do believe in being very involved with their social lives. We like for them to be social. When they are in a social situation, they get to really see the guy they thought was some good-looking hunk. Eventually, he will open his mouth and say something stupid, and they will see it. That happens all the time. They will realize that, while none of us are perfect, we should be able to recognize the difference between good and evil.

"Dad, You Were Right"

One day when I was out of town, I called home and talked with one of my kids, who said, "Dad, we went out to the ball game with Such-and-such and So-and-so. Do you know what they said? Dad, you were right!"

I don't know how many times I have heard these words: "Gee, Dad, you were right."

Several months ago I remember coming home and hearing, "Dad, So-and-so's going with So-and-so."

My response was: "I give it three months, honey. I like those kids, but it isn't serious. It's just temporary puppy love."

"But, Dad, it *is* serious."

"Believe me, honey, they aren't serious. I've been there and I know what I'm talking about."

Sure enough, within two months, they had broken up and I was told, "Dad — you were right."

"Honey," I said, "I didn't come in on the pumpkin wagon. I've been your age before."

"I'm Trying To Say Yes"

All I want to do in this book is to get parents to seek God's wisdom in His Word.

We have to create a situation and an atmosphere where our young people can get together. If you say, "I don't know how," then pray and ask God. He will show you.

You can't always be saying to your kids, "No! You can't! Don't! Stop!" They will just rebel against that kind of negativity. You have to find positive things that they can do.

I have sat down with my children and said to them, "I have predetermined in my mind that every time you ask me something I'm trying every way I can to say yes."

Before that, I always tried to say no just because that's what I wanted to do. Have you ever done that as a parent? I would say, "No, bless God, you have no business doing that! Why? Because I said so!" That doesn't make much sense, and it won't carry much weight down the road.

So, I tell my kids that I am trying to find a way to say yes every time they ask me something; then when I say something that I mean, it carries much more weight.

In relationships, we parents have to teach our children how to pick out friends or they will never know how to pick out a lifetime mate. We have to tell them the truth. If we don't do that, they will believe the lies they hear from somebody else. Remember that.

14

Teaching Kids About Sex

The time will come — if not already — when your child will want to know about sex. You need to realize that he will find out about it from somebody, so it had better be from you. You must be willing to take the time to teach him about sex, but it isn't something you can do in five minutes.

One time at a men's retreat I remember a dad saying to me, "Well, we had the meeting last night."

"What meeting?" I asked.

"With my boy. I talked to him about the birds and the bees."

"Really? Did you get everything said?"

"Oh, yeah, we covered it all."

"Do you think your boy understood it?"

"No problem. It wasn't nearly as hard as I thought it would be. But, thank God, that's over!"

My response to him was: "I guarantee you, Dad, you aren't done; you've just started. You've opened the lid to the box, but nothing has even come out yet."

Children don't need to be reading articles from magazines like *Redbook*, *Cosmopolitan* and *Woman's Day* to find out about human sexuality. They need to be talking to men and women of God about it, specifically their parents.

God is the One Who created sex, but people seem to act as if they think the devil did it. Sometimes I feel that Christians just let their heads go out to lunch on this subject. Most of us as parents don't really know how to talk with our children about sex, mostly because our parents probably didn't talk with us about it or their parents with them. It can be uncomfortable.

Dad says to his son, "Do you know what to do?"

"Oh, yeah, Dad; I know all about it."

"Well, that's good. But you had better not ever do it!"

"Don't worry, Dad."

All I can say is, we parents had better have more to say about it than that!

Suppose Mom is standing at the sink doing the dishes and her kid asks her a question about sex. She can't be shocked and just drop a plate or pass out right there. She has to keep herself under control in order to handle the situation correctly.

Parent, be careful not to overreact when faced with your child's question about sex. Just act normal and stay calm and simply answer the question you have been asked.

Make Your Answer Fit the Hearer

If it's your five-year-old asking the question, give an answer a five-year-old can understand. If your ten-year-old asks it, give an answer a ten-year-old can understand. Don't answer your kid the same way you would talk with a twenty-five-year-old. It isn't necessary that you go into a five-hour dissertation, using all kinds of graphs and charts. Just tell your kid what he needs to know and let that be all for now.

One year I was attending a Christian conference in Springfield, Missouri. At one of the meetings a professor gave a good session on the subject of teaching our children about sex. He took questions from the audience and just talked with us.

At one point he made this statement: "When talking to your kids about sex, don't be making up names for parts of the anatomy, like calling the penis a 'ying-ying' or 'wing-wang.' Call body parts what they are."

That's when this lady stood up and said, "Professor, I have a problem with what you just said."

"What?" he asked.

"I can't say that word."

"What word?"

"The word you just told us to use."

"You mean *penis?*"

"That's the word!"

"What's your problem, ma'am?"

"Well, I have a seven-year-old son, and I'm just wondering what I need to do."

"If you don't call it that," he said, "what do you call it?"

"I call it 'his turtle,'" she said.

Her statement brought down the house! It took a moment for the speaker to compose himself and be able to continue with his discussion.

Ignorance About Sex

Now as a school administrator, I have seen junior-high boys get so embarrassed about sex. You might be shocked at how ignorant most of our kids are. You may think they know everything about it; but they don't really know anything — nobody has ever told them!

I have dealt with kids who are as ignorant as can be about sex because their parents wouldn't talk to them about it. We read stories all the time about girls who have babies without even knowing they were pregnant; some don't have the slightest idea how they got pregnant.

Now you may think there is no way that could ever happen with so much information available, but it happens all the time.

Some girls will say, "Well, I did so-and-so and thought that would keep me from getting pregnant." That's ignorance gone to seed!

Children don't know about sex because their parents haven't talked to them about it. Why? Because their parents don't know how. But it's time we find out how.

God Made Sex To Be Good

Did you know there is reference to sex all through the Bible?

Now when I am talking to parents about teaching their children, the first thing I say to them is: "Don't lie to your kids."

God made sex and He made it to be good. But the devil is working hard against it because it's so precious to God. Don't let the world teach your children and make sex sound perverted. Virginity and the sexual act of marriage were set up by God. The world system is working against our children, trying to pervert sex every way that it can.

In the 1870s, the average girl first menstruated when she was 16 or 17; today, she is more likely to begin at 12 or 13. The average age of puberty in 1870 was 16.5; today, it is 12.5. The average marriage age then was 18; today, it is 22.8. The average length of time between puberty and marriage in those days was about two years; today, it is at least ten years. The main reason today's young people are maturing sexually at an earlier age is because our general health is better. When you combine such factors as earlier sexual maturity and later marriage with media pressure and a breakdown of the American family, which has many teenagers desperately looking for a close relationship, it is no surprise that young people are so vulnerable to sexual sin.[1]

I have a way to combat this: it's called the truth of God's Word.

When talking to parents, I say: "When your kids ask you about sex, don't lie to them. Sit down with them, talk with them and tell them the truth. Tell them that sex is good and that moms and dads love having sex. Tell them that sex is a wonderful part of marriage. But then tell them that because God did not intend for people to have sex outside of marriage, doing so is dangerous and will bring consequences."

If parents will say something like that, it might make their children think before getting themselves in a mess.

Sex Is Like the Ark of God

In 2 Samuel 6, there is the story of David having the ark of the covenant brought back to Jerusalem. The ark was a very special box that contained the glory, the power and the awesome wonder of Almighty God.

As mentioned in verse 5, they were bringing the ark back to Jerusalem. David and the people were singing, dancing, slapping their tambourines and having themselves a joyous time. Then all of a sudden, the oxen hit a bump in the road and the box began to fall, so a man named Uzzah reached out to stop the box from falling to the ground. But the moment he touched that box, he dropped dead as a doornail! (See vv. 6,7.)

I can imagine how that must have caused everybody to stop all their singing and dancing. Standing around, one person asks, "What happened?" Another says, "I don't know — he touched the box and just dropped dead."

---

[1] McDowell and Day, *Why Wait*, p. 56.

At that point David is afraid, so he decides against taking the ark into the city. Consider what happens next. David turns aside to a farmhouse that was owned by a man named Obed-edom the Gittite. Their conversation may have sounded something like this:

The farmer comes to the door and says, "Yes? What is it?"

"My name is David. I am the king at Jerusalem. We were coming by, and we have this box here."

Obed-edom asks, "What box?"

"It's God's house. He lives there in that box. I want to know if we can leave it in your living room?"

Obed-edom yells to his wife, "Martha, come here a minute! Is it okay if they leave that box here with us?"

"Sure. Bring it on in," she says.

Then David gives him a warning: "Whatever you do, don't touch that box. Don't even dust it. We have a problem with it, and we need to figure out what to do."

So Obed-edom says, "Okay. Bring it on in." Then he says, "Now, Martha, don't touch that box. I don't care how dusty it gets."

Verse 11 tells us how the ark was left there for three months. David goes on to Jerusalem and tries to find out what went wrong. Then something happens. He gets word from Obed-edom, who says, "I want you to come and get that box!"

"What's the problem?"

"Ever since you left it at my place, my sheep, camels and cattle have increased, and the dung is piled up to my eyeballs! Get that box out of here!" (As 2 Samuel 6:12 says, **The Lord hath blessed the house of Obed-edom, and all that pertaineth unto him, because of the ark of God.**)

The box where God lived was meant to bring blessing, abundant protection and provision. Obed-edom just had it there in his living room. He wasn't praying and asking it to do a thing;

he was just watching it. But verse 12 tells how the blessing of God overtook him because of the ark. And that's the same box that caused another man to drop dead.

That's the way I think of sex. Sex was created by God for marriage. It's a most wonderful thing, a part of the marriage relationship. But when used outside of marriage, it will cause you to die. It can kill you mentally, emotionally, socially and physically.

You see, David figured out why that happened with the box: he didn't read the instructions. God meant for the box to be handled in a certain way, but it wasn't handled the way God had said and, as a result, Uzzah fell dead.

When David went back and read the scroll, one of the instructions said, "Don't touch the box." David thought, *That's an important point. If I had read that, I would have known not to touch the box.*

No Sex Before Marriage!

So in teaching your children about sex, don't lie to them, but say: "Sex is one of the greatest things that ever happened to the marriage relationship. You're going to love it, but don't mess with it. It was created by God. If you handle it wrong, you could die."

I tell young people that it's God's will, God's best for them to wait to have sex after marriage and to have sex only with their spouse. Then it will be great. But having sex before marriage will kill them. It's sin!

When telling that to young people, I can almost see the fear of God come on them — and that's exactly what I want.

Some kids start snickering when talking about sex. But if you have told your kids the truth, they aren't going to be caught up in all those snickers. They know what sex is and what it isn't; and they will come to see it as just a part of life.

I highly recommend that you take all the time needed to talk to your kids about sex. Maybe you don't know where to start; maybe you don't know all the terminology. There are some great books on sex that you can find in Christian bookstores to help you teach your children about it.

Remember, the devil is working on your kids every day, but he is a liar. Don't let your kids be led away by listening to his lies. The way you stop those lies is with the truth, and the truth comes first from the Bible and then from a knowledgeable book on human sexuality.

There are two great books on this subject which I would recommend: *Sex Education Is for the Family* by Tim LaHaye and *How To Help Your Child Say No to Sexual Pressure* by Josh McDowell. They are available through your local Christian bookstore.

15

Marital Conflict

Now the whole idea behind friendship is that eventually people are headed toward the goal of choosing a lifetime mate.

If our kids can't even pick out a good friend, how will they ever be able to pick out a lifetime mate?

Lots of kids don't have any friends because they are trying so hard to pick out a mate. It's like they are jumping from square one to square twelve and are missing everything in between. But it won't work that way.

The First Sin and Its Consequences

Now I want us to look at what happened in Genesis 3. This isn't a very edifying chapter; it's about what took place in the beginning when God's curses were spoken into existence.

Adam and Eve had just sinned against God's commandments, so they were hiding from Him.

Then God came down and asked where Adam was. Now don't ever think God didn't know where Adam was; He knew *exactly* where Adam was. But He wanted Adam to respond.

Finally, Adam said, "I'm here, Lord."

"What are you doing, Adam?"

"I'm hiding." (See v. 10.)

Then God pressed Adam, asking what the problem was, so Adam said: "It's that wife You gave me, Lord. Everything was going well until You gave her to me. She made me eat some of that fruit — the one You told me not to eat. She did it, Lord, and she's hiding over there. You ought to go talk to her." (Author's paraphrase; see v. 12.)

So God went over to her and said, "Eve, what happened?"

"Well, Lord, it's like this: Everything was going along really smooth. But You know that snake You made? He came in here and told me a bunch of lies. If You hadn't made that snake, Lord, this never would have happened. He lied to me and tricked me into eating that fruit. It's all his fault!" (Author's paraphrase; see v. 13.)

God then went over to the serpent and spoke a curse to him, saying: "Serpent, you are cursed above every animal. You are going to crawl on your belly and eat dust the rest of your life." (See v. 14.)

Then He turned back to Adam and Eve and began telling them what would happen as the result of their sin. He said to them, "Adam, you are going to have to work by the sweat of your brow; and, Eve, you are going to have pain in childbirth." (See vv. 16-19.)

Marital Conflict — A Result of Sin

I want us to look specifically at Genesis 3:16, where God said to the woman:

I will greatly multiply thy sorrow and thy conception; in sorrow thou shalt bring forth children; and thy desire shall be to thy husband, and he shall rule over thee.

The last portion of this verse is a strange statement for God to put in with all these curses. Again, He says:

...and thy desire shall be to thy husband, and he shall rule over thee.

God was saying, "By the way, part of the curse in sin is that the wife is going to desire her husband, and he shall rule over her."

This doesn't make much sense when you read it in the *King James Version*, so let me explain what this part of God's curse really means. Basically, it's saying:

"Mister, here's what will happen now that sin is on this planet: You will find a wife, get married and go away on your honeymoon. But then one morning as you are getting ready for work, you will grab a pair of pants and shove one leg inside them. Then you will stand up and try to shove your other leg down the other side. But there will be a problem. When shoving your leg down the other side, you will find that somebody else already has her leg inside those pants. Both you and your wife will be trying to wear the pants in the family!"

A major result of sin is marital conflict. Whenever two people get married without Jesus in their lives, they are destined for a rocky marriage. That is part of the curse which said (author's paraphrase): "Woman, your husband will rule over you, which means because of the sin nature in you, your desire will be to rule over him." This is where we get women's liberation — women wanting to take the place of men.

God was saying, "Women, your desire will be to rule over your husbands and, men, you shall rule over your wives."

The two clauses of Genesis 3:16 — *Thy desire shall be to thy husband* and *he shall rule over thee* — are in contrast to each other. These are antithetical in the Hebrew sentence structure.[1] Thus, sin destroyed the marriage harmony.

This is where male chauvinism comes from.

---

[1] F. J. ANDERSON, *THE SENTENCE IN BIBLICAL HEBREW* (THE HAGUE, NETHERLANDS: MOUTON, 1974), P. 150.

Men don't really know how to treat their wives. They want to rule like Attila the Hun, saying, "I'm the biggest and the smartest, so I'm in charge!" The truth is, men who act like that are the dumbest!

So what we have here is a situation where two people supposedly "feel in love" when actually what they have is a desire for one another's flesh. They seem to enjoy laughing together and going places together, so they get married. Then after being married a while, they start fighting like cats and dogs.

That marital conflict is the result of their sin nature. They need to be redeemed from that sin nature, and the Redeemer's name is Jesus. They have to ask forgiveness and be covered by His blood. Then they will have power over the sin in their lives.

Without that, they will never be able to experience a good marriage. I don't care how much they felt in love or how many dates they had in the beginning. It doesn't matter how many roses or boxes of candy he sent to her or how many valentine cards they exchanged. It's impossible for them to have a truly good marriage if they are living without Jesus!

Only ten percent of people in America — one out of ten households in our country — live in a home where the father is the primary breadwinner and the mother stays home with the children. That means ninety percent of us are living in a different situation, which can create some challenges.[2]

Who Really Wears the Pants?

At one church I had attended, there was a counselor on staff. Both he and his wife had been married and divorced before they met one another. Then they met at church, were married and were serving God while working on the church staff.

He told me about an experience that had occurred between them. He said:

---

[2] Howard G. Hendricks, *Heaven Help the Home* (Wheaton, Illinois: Victor, 1973,1990), p. 12.

"My new bride has two sons from her previous marriage. They really liked me, and it was a tremendous relationship. We had been married for a couple of weeks when one morning we all were sitting at the kitchen table, eating our Cheerios. My new wife had found some reason to disagree with me over an issue, and she was really letting me have it verbally.

"When I had taken all I could, I told her I didn't mind her wearing the pants in the family, but she should let me get out of them first. Then I pushed back from the table, unbuttoned and unzipped my pants, dropped them to the floor, stepped out of them and handed them over to her. Then I sat back down and finished eating my Cheerios."

Know the Truth

God loves for males and females to get together. He made it that way for a man and a woman. It was His idea in the beginning.

But if we don't follow certain rules, devastation will occur. The world and the devil are always working against us. If we don't go to church and stay full of God's Word, our flesh will be working against us, too. That means, "Three strikes and we're out!"

So often, young people think they have fallen in love when they couldn't spell the word if you gave them four letters. They need to be taught some things about life. But they don't need to learn it from the world; they need to learn it from their moms and dads, who tell them the truth. It's the truth that sets us free and keeps us free. (John 8:32.)

16

Lives Committed to God

Sometimes people will look at me and say, "Joe, with the number of kids that you have, aren't you worried about living in today's times?"

"No. Why should I be?"

"Well, you know, there are all kinds of things going on these days. I mean, you have all those daughters, and it looks as if everybody in America will have AIDS. There won't be a man left who is a virgin that a girl could marry."

"Sure there will be," I say. "We prayed before our daughters were ever conceived, and I believe there are five godly men being trained up right now to marry them someday, and there is a godly young woman for my son."

When I say that, some people just look at me in disbelief.

I remember having a conversation like this with one person while we were standing in the hallway there at school. That person looked at me as if there were just no way that could ever happen.

Another person was getting somewhat angry about what I was saying and wondered how somebody would even want to believe that way.

In response, I said: "As Psalm 112:1,2 says, if I fear the Lord and delight greatly in His commandments, my children will be mighty upon the earth, and I believe what my Bible says. I know my children can be klutzy sometimes and they can mess up, but they're going to be mighty. I didn't just make up that statement; God said it."

"But how are they going to survive, Joe? Dear God, don't you think this economy is bad?"

"Well, as my Bible says, wealth and riches will be in their house, so I don't care what happens to the economy." (See Ps. 112:3.)

Knowing the Good Makes You Recognize the Evil

Now as mentioned earlier in our study, Daniel and those other boys were taken into captivity by King Nebuchadnezzar. They were made slaves; yet they prospered up to their eyeballs.

A few years ago when we took our children to Washington, DC, we went to the mint and watched money being made. That day they were producing $20 bills, and we saw pallets of those bills lined up there.

Our tour guide told us that in one room FBI agents were being trained to spot counterfeit money. That's their specialty. They go through several weeks of training, but not once in the entire program do they see a counterfeit bill. They spend those three weeks studying the good ones; then they will know the counterfeit when they see it.

I have been some places in this country where people are trying to teach their kids all about the evil in this world. They say, "We have to teach them about things like suicide, drugs and sexual promiscuity and how they are so bad."

When visiting with one youth group, I asked about the films they had been shown, and they said they saw a graphic film on suicide. (For heaven's sake, my kids don't need to know about suicide; they wouldn't think of killing themselves.)

You might say, "We need to teach them about drugs. They have to know how it's done so that they won't do it."

No, they don't!

That's what happened in the Garden of Eden. Adam and Eve knew the goodness of God; they didn't know the evil. But the moment they took the forbidden fruit, they could see the evil. That's when they had to leave the garden.

I'm not saying we should never be teaching our children about pitfalls to avoid, but we have to use wisdom.

Our Kids Need To Know God's Word

Our kids don't need to be taught the evil; they need to be taught the pure and good Word of God. Then when they see something evil, they will say, "That's evil; I can tell by looking at it." Why? "Not because I have studied evil, but because I know what the good is." We want them to know the good.

Our kids need to know that God's vision for them is good for all of their lives. They may say: "But God won't do anything for me. I'll be poor and ugly and will probably marry an ugly person because God wants me to. Besides, all the good ones are getting married off, so there won't be anybody who I would want left for me!"

That's a lie! God said He would give us the desires of our hearts. (Ps. 37:4.) God has good plans for us. But if we don't read His Book, we won't know that. He says He will do above and beyond all we ask or think. (Eph. 3:20.) Jesus wants to be Lord over our social lives just as much as any other area.

Remember, if Jesus tarries, we parents must be teaching our next generation about the church and about the principles of God's Word. Our children must then go on to do more than we have done — and they will.

235

We Must Develop the Life of Jesus in Our Kids

Our job is simple. All we have to do is develop within our kids the four things Jesus developed in His life here on earth.

First, we must plant God's *vision* inside them.

Second, we must see that they are *disciplined*.

Third, we must teach them that they aren't morons but are *gifted to succeed* in this life here on earth.

Fourth, we must teach them the value of true *friendship* — how to be a true friend to others, how to have others be true to them in their relationships throughout life and how to get along with both friends and enemies.

Perfection in This Life Is a Myth

As I have told my children: "My love and God's love for you are not based on whether you are a straight-A student or you make the basketball team. We love you just as you are. Success will come to you if you stay diligent because God has put within you the ability to succeed, and you will be successful in some area of life."

The world acts like perfection is for everybody and is constantly painting a picture of perfection. Every advertisement on TV shows people around the house dressed up like they are headed for church. You never see a commercial for dish soap in a dirty house. They work hard at presenting a false picture of perfection.

But we aren't perfect. We are righteous. We are forgiven. We will fall down at times, but we are to get back up again. (Prov. 24:16.)

When we keep getting up, it really frustrates the devil to no end. He says, "I thought I knocked them down, but they're standing up again!" He keeps trying to mess us up and is always wanting us to feel guilty.

But I say to him: "There is no condemnation to those who are in Christ Jesus[1], and I happen to be in Christ Jesus right now. So, devil, you have to take it up with Him!"

Then I get up again and keep on moving. I want my children to do that too.

"What happened, son?"

"I fell down, Dad."

"That's all right, son. Just get back up again. Let's repent to God, get our hands back on the plow and get moving again."

This applies to children in every area of their lives, whether on the basketball court, in academics, in relationships with their parents and friends, or just life in general.

God isn't saying to anyone, "You deserve to fall down; you've been sinning." God never says that to anybody who has sinned. He keeps saying to us: "Repent and get up. I'm not mad at you. I have never been mad at you and never will be; I love you. So repent, get up and go on with life."

It's important that we live this same way toward our children.

Be Their Number-One Cheerleader

We have to be the number-one cheerleader in our homes. You can be, and I believe you will be.

If you have read all the way through this book, perhaps you have learned more about your job as a parent. Let me tell you what I think you need to do now.

These days we have heard plenty of truth being preached in our good churches. What God wants us to do now is to *act* on what we know. We have to be a living example to other people, especially our children, of what God says in His Word. Sometimes

---

[1] ROMANS 8:1.

237

it's good for us to confess boldly before others that Jesus is the Lord and Savior of our lives.

Now I want to give you the opportunity to make an outward show of commitment to God. If you are willing to do so, pray this:

Father, in the name of Jesus, I come to You and I confess that, as a parent, I realize I can do nothing without Jesus, but that with Him all things are possible.

The enemy has come as the accuser of the brethren to make me, as a parent, feel guilty for doing things I should not have done and for failing to do the things I should have done. He has tried to make me feel guilty for saying things to my children I should not have said and for failing to say the things I could have said.

So, Father, I ask You now, in accordance with Your Word in First John 1:9, to forgive me of any sins I have committed against You, against my family, against my fellowman or even against my own flesh. I thank You for washing me clean by the blood of Your Son, Jesus, and for taking my sins from me as far as the east is from the west.

I refuse to let the devil hold me in the past any longer.

Father, give me wisdom as a parent to train up my child in the way he should go.

For my child, I ask three things:

First: Teach my child to fear You!

Psalm 34:11 — **Come, ye children, hearken unto me: I will teach you the fear of the Lord.**

Proverbs 9:10 — **The fear of the Lord is the beginning of wisdom....**

Proverbs 3:16 — **Length of days is in her (wisdom's) right hand; and in her left hand riches and honour.**

As You have said in Your Word, the fear of the Lord is the beginning of wisdom, and with that wisdom will come long life, wealth, riches and honor to my child.

Second: Surround my child with the shield of divine favor.

Psalm 5:12 — For thou, Lord, wilt bless the righteous; with favour wilt thou compass him as with a shield.

John 16:33 — Jesus said, ...In the world ye shall have tribulation: but be of good cheer; I have overcome the world.

Luke 6:28 — Bless them that curse you, and pray for them which despitefully use you.

In the world there are those who would want to use or abuse my children, so help my children to do righteously and surround them with a shield of divine favor. Just as Joseph and Daniel were in captivity — being the wrong culture, wrong color, wrong language, wrong religion; having no friends, no family, no finances, no influence — they both ended up running the very countries that took them captive. May my children know Your favor.

Third: Send godly friends into my children's lives who will sharpen them like iron and cause them to be all You want them to be.

Proverbs 27:17 NIV — As iron sharpens iron, so one man sharpens another.

Proverbs 13:20 — He that walketh with wise men shall be wise: but a companion of fools shall be destroyed.

Proverbs 14:7 — Go from the presence of a foolish man, when thou perceivest not in him the lips of knowledge.

Father, there are over one hundred Scriptures in the Word of God relating to friends and friendship. I know how important friendships are to my children, so I thank You now for bringing godly friends into their lives.

I pray this for my kids in Jesus' name, and I give You all the praise and honor and glory for bringing it to pass in their lives.

Conclusion

Much could have been written here that wasn't. I certainly did not exhaust the subject of parenting. I could have given dozens more Scriptures and illustrations in this book. But the point has been made: God has the answers.

You see, there are no perfect parents, and I certainly don't consider myself an expert on parenting. My kids will quickly back up this fact. But that's okay since perfection is not a prerequisite for having children.

My goal has been to put hope back into the lives of moms and dads, So, I leave you with two thoughts:

1. You cannot do anything about the past except to repent. Once that is done, then it is time to start growing in the grace and knowledge of our Lord Jesus Christ. We are going to be doers of the Word. If we fall, we have to get back up. ...**All things are possible to him that believeth** (Mark 9:23).

2. Biblical parenting does not come about by the changes we force on our children but by the changes we allow God to make in us. A child when fully taught will be just like his teacher. (Luke 6:40, AMP.)

God bless you and your family as you grow in Him.

Prayer for Salvation

You can make Jesus Christ your Lord and Savior, receive God's help now in this life and be saved from eternal damnation.

The Bible says: **That if thou shalt confess with thy mouth the Lord Jesus, and shalt believe in thine heart that God hath raised him from the dead, thou shalt be saved. For with the heart man believeth unto righteousness; and with the mouth confession is made unto salvation** (Rom. 10:9,10).

To receive Jesus Christ as the Lord and Savior of your life, sincerely pray this prayer from your heart:

Dear Heavenly Father,

I know that I have sinned and fallen short of Your expectations of me. I have come to realize that I cannot run my own life. I don't want to continue the way I have been living; neither do I want to face an eternity of torment or damnation.

I know the wages of sin is death, but I can be spared from this through the gift of the Lord Jesus Christ. I believe that Jesus is Your Son, that He died for me and that He rose from the dead on the third day. I confess that I am a sinner and that I need Your love and forgiveness. Come into my life, Jesus; forgive my sins and give me eternal life. I now confess Jesus as my Lord, and I thank You, Father, for my salvation.

I will not be ashamed of Jesus, and I will tell my friends and family members that I have made this wonderful decision. I will do my very best to chase after You and to learn Your ways by submitting to a pastor, by reading my Bible, by going to a church that preaches about You and by keeping sin out of my life.

I also ask You to give me the power to be healed from any sickness and disease in my body and to deliver me from those things that have me bound.

I love You and thank You, Father, for receiving me, and I look forward to a long and wonderful relationship with You, in Jesus' name. Amen.

About the Author

Joe McGee knows how to motivate and minister to people. Having served as leader of the Christian Education Department at Grace Fellowship in Tulsa, Oklahoma, and as administrator of its 500-student Christian school, he has taught numerous seminars and workshops on subjects ranging from children's ministry to marriage to Christian school management. In 1992 Joe was named to *Who's Who Among America's Teachers*.

Joe maintains a brisk speaking schedule and is a popular conference speaker, delighting audiences of all ages with his unique mixture of humor and inspiration.

During the past decade, Joe has traveled across America, preaching on a subject for which he has become best known: biblical parenting. As the father of six, Joe shares wisdom gained from his years of experience as husband, father, children's minister and school administrator. His insight, through a personable, warm and humorous presentation, has helped many families to rekindle hope for their lives through the knowledge of God's Word.

Joe's wide range of past experiences include serving as chapter president of the Full Gospel Businessmen's Fellowship, coordinator for his church's Cub Pack and Boy Scout Troop, county chairman of his political party, site visit chairman and commissioner for the International Christian Accrediting Association and crusade coordinator for Willie George Ministries.

Joe makes his home in Tulsa, Oklahoma, together with his wife, Denise, and their six children.

Audiovisual Materials by Joe McGee

Audio Cassette Messages

Biblical Parenting 101

Man: Lover, Leader, Provider

The Virtuous Woman From a Man's View

Training and Controlling Your Children

God's Vision for Your Family

How Kings Are Made

Parenting Your Teenager

Marriage Building 101

From Friendships to Dating

Passing On the Faith

Teaching Your Children About Sex

Your Child's Money

Your Child's Education

Video Cassette Messages

Biblical Parenting 101 (two ninety-minute tapes)

Marriage Building 101 (three tapes)

Other titles are available.

Seminars by Joe McGee

Seminars

Biblical Parenting 101: Vision, Discipline, Stewardship, Friendship

Marriage Builder 101: Communication, Money, Sex, Children

Men's Advance: Male vs. Female, Becoming Lover, Leader, Provider

Children's Workers Training: Organizing and Administrating Children's Ministry in the Local Church (Prayer, Preparation, Program and People)

Christian School Management: In-Service Training. Administrator as Manager; Parent and Student Issues; Staff Management and Motivation; Managing School Facility; Ministry Relationships

Each of these Seminars is taught in four ninety-minute sessions, running Friday through Sunday, or Sunday through Tuesday.

However, they may be condensed or expanded to meet your specific needs, such as a one-day conference on Saturday.

To request a catalog of available materials
or to obtain information on having Joe
minister in your community, contact:

Joe McGee Ministries
P. O. Box 691498
Tulsa, Oklahoma 74169-1498
800-482-5862
FAX (918) 482-5036

Please include your prayer requests and comments when you write.